A BRIEF THEOLOGY
OF
REVELATION

A BRIEF THEOLOGY
OF
REVELATION

The 1993 Warfield Lectures

Colin E. Gunton

t &t clark

T&T Clark

A Continuum imprint

The Tower Building
11 York Road
London
SE1 7NX

15 East 26th Street
Suite 1703
New York
NY 10010

First published 1995
This edition 2005

ISBN 0–5670–4111–5

British Library Cataloguing-in-Publication Data
A catalogue record for this book is available from the British Library

Typeset by Waverley Typesetters, Galashiels
Printed and bound in England by Cromwell Press, Wiltshire

For my parents

Contents

Preface

The doctrine of revelation has been in recent times at once neglected and overused. It has suffered neglect for reasons to do with the criticism of orthodox Christian belief both before and after Kant, when even the labours of Hegel were not enough to prevent its relative neglect into the early years of the twentieth century. The overemployment of the category arose in the course of a proper reaction to the neglect, particularly in Barth's attempts to overcome the epistemological challenges presented him by his predecessors and to allow the God of Jesus Christ to come to rational expression on his own terms. But it was, I believe, an overemployment, and resulted in an imbalance in the systematic structure of Barth's theology, as well as in those that were influenced by him. Some of the reasons for this will be set out in the course of the following lectures.

The imbalance generated by the attempt to retrieve the doctrine after centuries of relative neglect in turn helped to produce oversimplifications of the situation in one or two of the studies of revelation written in the years following Barth's and Bultmann's years of influence around the middle of the century, so that the time was ripe for the challenge represented by Ronald Thiemann's *Revelation and Theology* in 1985. These lectures were not written in direct response to Thiemann, although his work has been an important source of ideas.

The opportunity to develop this book came as a result of an invitation to deliver the 1993 Warfield lectures at Princeton

Theological Seminary.   To the honour of the invitation was added the generosity of the Seminary's hospitality and warmth of its welcome. The President, Dr Thomas Gillespie, and his colleagues and students ensured that the visit was a memorable one, and I am most grateful. Debts of gratitude are owed also to others, in the first place to many generations of Master's degree students at King's College, whose has been the doubtful privilege of enabling me to develop a theology of revelation while teaching a course in the subject. All of the chapters have received a hearing at seminars and conferences of the King's College Research Institute in Systematic Theology, and I am grateful to the students and colleagues – among them Christoph Schwöbel, Brian Horne, Francis Watson and Paul Helm – who have commented and criticised. Particular thanks must go to Alan Torrance who, in his busy first months at this institution found the time to read the chapters and write a set of comments which have been of great value in the process of revision.

COLIN GUNTON
King's College, London
Passiontide, 1994

Lecture 1

'A revealed religion?':
The problem of revelation
in modern theology

I *The problem of immediacy*

In a recent article in the *New York Review of Books* the biologist R. C. Lewontin considered some recent discussions of the possibility of what can only be called industrialised genetics. Not only did he ridicule the metaphysical claims of some of the scientists – for example, the attributing of agency to DNA, which is among the most inert of molecules – but he suggested that there is a more sinister side to the developments. Much potential profit is involved, and there is also a kind of inverted religion implicit in the claims that are made, for example in the use of the expression 'the biological grail'. 'It is a sure sign of their alienation from revealed religion that a scientific community with a high concentration of East European Jews and atheists has chosen for its central metaphor the most mystery-laden object of mediaeval Christianity.'[1]

That article is revealing in many ways, and not only for its recognition that religious and anti-religious assumptions shape the theories of scientists. What, however, is particularly interesting is the use of that expression, 'revealed religion'. What a scientist can use quite unselfconsciously, the theologian

[1] R. C. Lewontin, 'The Dream of the Human Genome', *New York Review of Books* 39 (28 May 1992), 31.

1

finds very difficult. Why are we embarrassed by the concept? That is the question to be explored in this lecture. There are today a number of religions and faiths purporting or believed to be revealed religions. On many understandings of the matter Judaism and Islam would count among them. But the naming of those two alongside Christianity immediately brings to mind the complexity of the topic. Even if there is *within* those faiths agreement as to the respects in which they are so described, there is certainly disagreement *between* them, and between them and Christianity. If we were to attempt to spell in what respects Judaism and Islam can be described as revealed religions or as religions of revelation, we should find distinctive differences between the two, though we should, to be sure, also have to be aware in making such judgements of the considerable differences internal to those faiths.

But the case of Christianity is far more complex, and not only for historical reasons. Certainly the historical reasons bulk large. Since the Reformation there have been major differences between Catholic and Protestant on the way in which Christianity is a revealed religion: on what is revealed, and how. The differences derive not only from beliefs about the nature of scripture and tradition, both of which will be the subject of future lectures. There is also at stake a far less easily formulable question about the nature of revelation according to Christianity, and its relation to its sources. There is almost certainly, for example, a much looser relationship between the church and the Bible than there is between Islam and the Quran. Recent times have made the matter still more complex, as we shall see.

It is a truism that since the Enlightenment the question of revelation has bulked large in Christian theology because that movement, if it can be so described, brought to the centre the epistemological dimension of belief. By tending to replace revelation by reason, or rather to displace it altogether, locating the source of revelation largely if not wholly in reason, it threw into question the historical basis of Christianity, and so opened up the modern debate about the epistemological basis of the faith. Hegel's contribution here is immense. From one point of view, he is a classic Enlightenment figure, standing for the absolute supremacy of reason, apparently against revelation. But because reason for him is the place of the dynamic self-revelation of God, he laid the ground for future developments, among them the theology of Barth. It is worth observing that for Hegel Christianity is the absolute, because it is the revealed religion.

Hegel's programme involved, and this was Kierkegaard's justified objection to it, the development of a form of immediacy. Indeed, the word 'immediate' (*unmittelbar*) appears repeatedly in the section of the *Phenomenology of Mind* in which the subject is treated. Three brief quotations will bring out the two points that should be noted:

> . . . this concrete God is beheld sensuously and immediately as a self, as a real individual human being . . .
>
> That Absolute Spirit has taken on the shape of self-consciousness inherently . . . [T]his appears now as . . . the belief that spirit exists in fact as a definite self-consciousness . . . that the believing mind *sees, feels* and *hears* this divinity.
>
> The divine nature is the same as the human, and it is this unity which is intuitively apprehended (*angeschaut*).[2]

The first point is that for Hegel revelation is the function of an immediate relation of God to the mind, just as for Schleiermacher religion is a form of immediacy to experience.[3] The second is that at the same time there is an ontological conflation of the divine and the human. Barth, we might say in anticipation of a later point, has bought into the first but not the second of these forms of immediacy: he appears to suppose, on the one hand, a form of revelational immediacy, while on the other to maintain a fundamental ontological difference between God and the world.

Since Hegel's time, theology has been dominated by quests for different forms of immediacy, and that, I believe, is one

[2] G. W. F. Hegel, *The Phenomenology of Mind*, translated by J. B. Baillie (London: George Allen & Unwin, 1949), pp. 758, 757, 760.

[3] That is not to say that for Schleiermacher God is necessarily understood as being immediate to experience. The answer to the question of whether and in what respect he tends to pantheism depends upon a decision about his concept of mediation.

root of our modern discomfort with the question of a revealed religion. The notion of a revealed religion, not as Hegel understood it but as some notion of the faith once for all delivered[4] to the saints (Jude 3) – notice that the idea is in some form biblical – has been replaced by different forms of immediacy. These can take forms that either dispense with revelation, or appear to have little constitutive role for it, as in Schleiermacher. But there is also a seeking of what can only be called a revelatory immediacy, a direct apprehension of the content of the faith that will in some way or other serve to identify it beyond question. The nineteenth-century quest for the essence of Christianity, the kernel within the husk, sought by the methods of biblical criticism, provides an obvious example.[5] But so do some forms of biblical fundamentalism – the truth straight out of the text – and, as Pannenberg has pointed out, the far from biblically fundamentalist theology of revelation of Karl Barth.[6] The various marks of this immediacy – if it is all of a single form – will, I hope, become clearer as the lecture proceeds.

In alluding to Pannenberg's criticism of Barth, I do not, as I hope will become apparent, wish to advocate Pannenberg's Hegelian alternative to Barth. There is, it can be argued, a quest for immediacy in Pannenberg's use of historical criticism to establish the resurrection that makes it rather like the nineteenth-century quest to find the essence of Christianity by historical means. (It is surely significant that, according to him, the resurrection, once established by historical-critical methods, means what it does self-

---

[4] παραδοθεῖσῃ. The character of the mediation implied in paradosis will concern us in a later lecture.

[5] The immediacy which that movement sought can be understood as one that freed the believer from the necessity of dependence on tradition.

[6] Pannenberg's concern is with the subjectivism he believes to be implicit in Barth's appeal to revelation. See, for example, *Systematic Theology Volume I*, translated by G. W. Bromiley (Edinburgh: T&T Clark, 1991), pp. 45–8. As we shall see in later lectures, it is possible to talk of different forms of mediation, and it might not be unjustified to say both that in Barth there is a kind of mediated immediacy and that Pannenberg's programme is an attempt to escape it through his concept of indirect revelation.

evidently).[7] Rather, I want to draw on a point made by Alan Spence in a recent paper on the theology of John Owen. Barth's insistence that God is revealed through God, he argues, detracts from the incarnational and pneumatological mediation of revelation. 'The underlying concept [sc. of Barth's position] is that revelation must be self-revelation and therefore only the divine nature can truly reveal God.'[8] Even if we concede to Barth the rejoinder he could make that revelation is mediated by the humanity of Christ,[9] we can continue to hold against him that the humanity is in some way given short measure, so that the mediatedness of revelation, given with the right hand, is in effect taken away by the left. Spence's conclusion surely has some justification: 'the breach implied here between the Word of God and Jesus the man can only be damaging for christology for it inevitably leads to the neglect of the historical life of Christ as the basis for our knowledge of God.'[10] We shall return to this question in later lectures.

Similar points can be made about the recent fashion for narrative or intratextuality. Is it not in some of its forms also a quest for immediacy, attempting an unmediated apprehension of revelation, even though its proponents would probably not put it that way? One problem seems to be the following. It must be conceded that there is a sense in which we are shaped by the narratives and other forms of language which form the context of our lives. But very near the surface in many 'postmodern' discussions of the matter is a suggestion of determinism, because they sometimes appear to imply that we are *created* or constituted by the texts. It is very likely, as John Lucas has argued in the case of theories of historical determinism, that such views are in any case self-refuting.[11] To

[7] Wolfhart Pannenberg, *Jesus – God and Man*, translated by L. Wilkins and D. Priebe (London: SCM Press, 1968), Chapter 3.

[8] Alan Spence, 'Christ's Humanity and Ours', Christoph Schwöbel and Colin E. Gunton, editors, *Persons, Divine and Human. King's College Essays in Theological Anthropology* (Edinburgh: T&T Clark, 1992), p. 89.

[9] Karl Barth, *Kirchliche Dogmatik* I/1 (Zürich: Evangelischer Verlag, 1944), p. 341: 'he remains free to be or not to be revealed in this form (*Gestalt*). The form here is that of the *humanitas Christi*.' Much hangs on the meaning of *Gestalt.*

[10] Spence, 'Christ's Humanity and Ours', p. 92.

[11] J. R. Lucas, *The Freedom of the Will* (Oxford: Clarendon Press, 1970).

speak about determination by narrative or text presupposes
the capacity to transcend constitution by the text, at least by
the person of the one who tells us of our constitution, so that
questions about the relation of word and reality, apparently
ruled out on some understandings of textuality, emerge in a
new form.

But the main question to be asked is theological. At a recent
discussion at which questions of this kind were being aired, a
neighbour turned to me and said: 'Is this not yet another form
of biblicism?' The context was the discussion of a paper by
Kenneth Surin, in which the following words appeared:

> Hence, these ('Christian') significations, this ('Christian') text,
> are properly to be regarded as the primary reality, the reality
> which subsumes that reality which is the world of 'common
> human experience'. But this primary reality is – textual. It is
> more than text, of course, but to understand what is at stake in
> saying that it is 'more than text' we have to await the *visio beatifica*,
> when the profane separation between word and thing will be
> healed.[12]

We are confident that we have passed the stage when we any
longer equate revelation and the actual words of Scripture,
but Surin suggests something remarkably like a modern-
sounding form of the same. Whether or not that is a form
of biblicism, and whether or not it is deterministic in its
implications, it certainly suggests a kind of revelatory
immediacy. Only in eternity shall we be able to transcend
determination by the text to discover whether or not reality is
more than text. What, then, on such an account is the relation
of Bible and revelation if it is not one of the forms of immediacy
that we have met?

We shall meet the problem of the Bible as revelation in the
fourth lecture. But before moving to the next section, I must
conclude this one by isolating the heart of the problem with
the fashionable alternative to traditional doctrines of the
revelatory character of biblical or dogmatic propositions. John
Baillie, in his study of revelation has claimed that in contrast

---

[12] Kenneth Surin, *The Turnings of Darkness and Light* (Cambridge: Cambridge
University Press, 1989), pp. 220–1.

to past beliefs, which held that revelation came in propositions
– either those of Catholic tradition or of Protestant Bible –
modern theology has come to a view that God 'reveals himself'.
But what is the status of this self-revelation? Is this another
suspicious form of immediacy? I think that it is. '[W]hat is
manifested or revealed is life; that this life is the overcoming
at once of death and of sin and so the final deliverance from
our ultimate human exigency.' Appropriately, he cites
Bultmann, theologian of existential immediacy: 'Revelation is
an event that destroys death, not a doctrine that death does
not exist . . .'.[13] Some kind of immediate experience appears
in modern times to have replaced a traditional view of the
mediation of the faith in propositional terms. That raises again
the question of the place of the much maligned proposition,
to which we now turn.

II *Unfair to propositions*

George Lindbeck's critique of what he calls the cognitive-
propositional conception of theology is in effect an attack on
the notion of revealed religion. As has been pointed out often
enough, he gains his point only by a very tendentious account
of the cognitive approach. 'For a propositionalist, if a doctrine
is once true, it is always true, and if it is once false, it is always
false.'[14] Against the implicit suggestion that propositionalism
is a kind of optional and vaguely reactionary or disreputable
position, it must be protested in the name of logic that it is as
a matter of fact the case that once something is true it is always
true.[15] That is not, however, the same as believing, as its
statement also appears to suggest, that doctrines, once
formulated, must always be expressed in the same precise form

[13] John Baillie, *The Idea of Revelation in Recent Thought* (New York: Columbia
University Press, 1956), pp. 55–6.
[14] George Lindbeck, *The Nature of Doctrine. Religion and Theology in a Postliberal
Age* (London: SPCK, 1984), p. 16.
[15] Paul Helm, *The Divine Revelation. The Basic Issues* (London: Marshall, Morgan
& Scott, 1982), to whom I owe some of the arguments of this section, provides a
clear example: 'The statement "God is good" is timelessly true since it does not
make sense to suppose that God might cease to be good . . .', p. 24.

of words. (That is to confuse a sentence with a proposition.) How a form of the propositionalist view can be held to be the case without denying all the other things that postmodernity expects us to believe I shall examine later. But let me first rehearse the kinds of objection that are made to cognitive propositionalism or to the view that Christianity is, in a sense to be explored, rightly described as a revealed religion.

One objection that need not detain us for long is that the propositionalist view represents a false theory of the relation of language to reality, namely, that there is a one-to-one correspondence between words and things. A reply to this is that it does not necessarily so suppose, and to hold so is to take the theory in its most wooden and indefensible form. Alister McGrath points out that even for those mediaevals who were proponents of theories most like the ones Lindbeck rejects, 'doctrines were reliable, yet incomplete descriptions of reality'. [16] Moreover, proponents of theories of metaphorical truth are far from supposing a naive one-to-one correlation of word and thing; yet one may with every right suppose that if it was once true that Achilles is a lion, it is always true (given that is, appropriately formulated time-indicators). Let me take an example that is nearer to our purposes. If it was once true that Jesus died for our sins on the cross, then it is always true. I take that sentence to be propositional, cognitive, in that it makes claims for the truth of that which lies beyond its formulation in words, and to form one dimension of what it is to claim that Christianity is a revealed religion. A variety of the assault on the cognitive nature of theological claims, the contention of Sallie McFague that it is 'idolatrous' to cling on to past formulations,[17] need also not detain us long. To hang on to language from the past may indeed smack of idolatry, or perhaps only of atavistic[18] conservatism, but the argument only

[16] Alister McGrath, *The Genesis of Doctrine. A Study in the Foundations of Doctrinal Criticism. The 1990 Bampton Lectures* (Oxford: Blackwell, 1990), pp. 16–17.

[17] Sallie McFague, *Metaphorical Theology. Models of God in Religious Language* (London: SCM Press, 1983), pp. 2–7. We might take as an example recent discussion of a claim that I hold to be part of Christianity's revealedness, that God is to be named as Father.

[18] I avoid the word 'patriarchal' because that is not in question here.

holds if there are reasons to believe that the past was wrong. Her argument, assuming as it does that theological language is essentially projected, begs the very question which is at issue. Does our language or does it not refer, or affect to refer, to realities which lie beyond it, however elusively? Does it or does it not affect to describe, albeit partially, obliquely and inadequately, those things which truly are? These seem to me to be the questions that Lindbeck, in some of his contentions, and some narrativists consistently evade.

The second objection to the propositional form is that it is intellectualist, reducing what is a teaching of salvation to merely abstract cognitive form. The charge is particularly strongly made in F. G. Downing's book, *Has Christianity a Revelation?*[19] His theses are that there is little evidence for the claim that the Bible gives knowledge of God, that revelation is an eschatological concept and best left there, and that the Bible offers a way of salvation rather than a form of knowledge. He does indeed raise there some very interesting questions about the nature of propositions, and particularly theological ones. It has to be conceded that there have been in the history of theology the development of propositions that appear to stand in rather tenuous relation to the nature of Christian faith, and, indeed, it is not only those who stand in the tradition of the Reformation who have sympathy with Melanchthon's famous disavowal of scholastic speculation. But that propositionalist theologian, John Calvin, knew better than to go any further, and provides evidence for the fact that the matter is more complex than propositional against non-propositional, intellectualist against existentialist. His conception of knowledge was far from being intellectualist in the narrow sense, though we can be grateful that he knew the value of clear thought and expression. The shape of his theology, from the beginning seeking to integrate the knowledge of God and of ourselves, is witness to theology as wisdom: not abstract, but saving and existentially relevant knowledge. But that wisdom had to be given cognitive form if it was to be worthy of belief.

[19] F. G. Downing, *Has Christianity a Revelation?* (London: SCM Press, 1964).

The appropriate rejoinder to claims of intellectualism like that of Downing is to be found in making a distinction between various forms of proposition.[20] Some propositions may be merely abstract, but the kind of ones with which theology is and has been centrally concerned are not. For instance, the Patristic slogan that the unassumed is the unhealed is scarcely an intellectualist formulation, though it makes cognitive claims in propositional form. From a similar but also rather different context, it is interesting to cite against Downing's experiential reading of scripture that of Brian Haymes. Haymes points out that one of the duties of biblical parents was to teach their children the knowledge of God. How can that be done without some form of cognitive, albeit partly narrative, discourse, identifying their God and the claims he has upon them? 'Hear, O Israel: the Lord our God is one Lord. . . . And these words which I command you this day shall be upon your heart; and you shall teach them diligently to your children . . .' (Dt. 6.4, 6). Haymes comments: 'To be taught these things about God was to have knowledge of God . . . It is this knowledge, rather than any particular "acquaintance experience" that is foundational for most of the people of Israel.'[21] If Haymes is right, and much of what he says can hardly be denied, the question arises of whether, in forgetting the fact that revelation is mediated by teaching and tradition – better, perhaps, teaching mediated by tradition – we have neglected a good part of our biblical heritage in favour of a rather Marcionite or Gnostic reading of scripture. While it would be ludicrous to tar all those whom I have mentioned with the Gnostic brush – though I would be prepared to have a good try with some of them – there is something suspicious about the kind of direct communication with God which experiential views of revelation, and sometimes even Barth's actualist conception, appear to presuppose.

---

[20] A non-intellectualist example is provided by Helm, *The Divine Revelation*, p. 24: 'There is a bull in the next field.'

[21] Brian Haymes, *The Concept of the Knowledge of God* (London: Macmillan, 1988), p. 89.

The third objection to the propositional form is that it is 'static'. To be static is to sin against the essence of what we today think important and modern, in the very best sense, of course. The expression, like so many modern shibboleths, is used in a variety of different ways, as a guide to conceptual correctness. Thus the charge is often ignorantly levelled against the categories of Chalcedon that they presuppose a static and not a modern dynamic view of reality. But that is not quite the point at issue here, which is rather that propositional forms, claimed to be true always because true once, appear to encase the faith in a rigid and unrevisable straitjacket. Of course, they can, and sometimes do, but that is not to say that it is necessarily the case. Once again, all hangs on what kind of propositions, and what we mean by 'static'.

Let me concede, in the first instance, that the static is in general undesirable, though when an aircraft is taking off I for the most part prefer the land beneath it to remain so. Similarly, there is much that is profoundly unhealthy in much of what passes for dynamism in the modern world: the relentless processes of change that drive people into neurosis and cause them to spend so much time changing working practices that little work is actually done. P. T. Forsyth caught the mood eighty years ago when he spoke of ours as 'an outworn age trying to narcotise with mere energies its moral fatigue'.[22] If we change the language a little, a rather different point can be made. We may not like the static, but for the most part the stable is profoundly to be welcomed. Unstable marriages threaten families, unstable societies the well-being of those within them. The stable is not the foe of the dynamic, but is the form that the dynamism of the universe takes. 'Thank God for hard stones; thank God for hard facts; thank God for thorns and rocks and deserts and long years. At least I know now that I am not the best or strongest thing in the world. At least I know now that I have not dreamed of everything.'[23]

---

[22] P. T. Forsyth, *The Principle of Authority* (London: Independent Press, 1952. First edition 1913), p. 393.

[23] Cited from G. K. Chesterton by Stephen R. L. Clark, 'Orwell and the Anti-Realists', *Philosophy* 67 (1992), 141–54 (149).

The heart of our problem is not the proposition, but our tenuous hold on the tradition. Modernity has made doubters of us all, has appeared to cut such a breach between ourselves and our credal past that we do not know whether there is a faith once delivered to the saints, or at least whether we may appeal to it. One example will illustrate the point. Recall what Karl Barth said about Anselm's attitude to the creed, recognising as he said it the difference between the ancient and the modern. For his predecessors, as for Anselm, there is an 'objective credo which compels Christian humility before the *ratio veritatis* that is the presupposition of all human knowledge of heavenly things'. There is, we might say, a revealed religion, a stable set of proposition-like affirmations on which he may base his theological enterprise. 'Anselm always has the solution of his problems already behind him (through faith in the impartial good sense of ecclesiastical authority), while, as it were, they are still ahead.'[24] There is stability for you, and yet not a static stability or one lacking in dynamic, because stability is not the same as inertia. Anselm achieved a theology that was in several important respects an advance on the thought of his predecessors and is still full of insight for the enquirer, and yet he lived in the pre-modern world in which propositional truth was accepted so naively. I labour the point, for it is important. The problem we face is the modern calling in question of the five aspects of the Christian faith that Anselm took for granted: Bible, creed, church, tradition and authority. The problem is not that the propositions with which we are concerned are static; it is that they have been called into question. And the five aspects set the scene for the remainder of these lectures: authority, Bible, tradition and church will concern us in future lectures, as mediators of revelation, for that is the problem we face. For the rest of this one, let me develop some thoughts on those repositories of propositional wisdom, the creeds; or rather, for it is a much better and broader way of putting the matter

---

[24] Karl Barth, *Fides Quaerens Intellectum. Anselm's Proof of the Existence of God in the Context of his Theological Scheme*, translated by I. W. Robertson (London: SCM Press, 1960), pp. 25–6.

– and one more in line with the Reformation tradition – on the confessions through which our faith has traditionally been articulated.

III   *Credal propositionality*

In this section, the chief concern will be to continue the discussion of the static and the stable, and to make some observations about the way in which confessional statements may be conceived to work, or not to work. The first thing to say is that although credal statements are to be understood, for the most part, as doxological affirmations, that is in no way inconsistent with saying that they contain propositions, claims that things are such and such and so not their contradictories. Let me take some examples, biblical and non-biblical. 'In the beginning, God created the heaven and the earth.' 'God is spirit.' 'The word became flesh, and dwelt among us.' 'But in fact Christ has been raised from the dead' (1 Cor. 15.20). 'Yet for us there is one God, the Father, from whom are all things and for whom we exist, and one Lord, Jesus Christ, through whom are all things and through whom we exist' (1 Cor. 8.6). 'Therefore he is the mediator of a new covenant' (Heb. 9.15). 'I believe in God the Father, Maker of heaven and earth.' 'We believe in the Holy Spirit, the Lord and giver of life.' 'Christ alone is God's own eternal Son, whereas we are accepted for his sake as children of God by grace.'[25] 'Jesus Christ, as he is attested to us in Holy Scripture, is the one Word of God which we have to hear . . .'[26] These affirmations have varying grammatical and logical form. Some describe events, or acts; others the status of those who act or bring about events. Yet for all their diversity, I would claim, simply as they stand, they are, or purport to be revelatory. They are components of a revealed religion. They are not chosen at random, and intentionally so, for it has always been held that some statements encapsulate the heart of the faith more appropriately than others. To state

---

[25] *The Heidelberg Catechism*, 33, in *Reformed Confessions of the 16th Century*, edited by Arthur C. Cochrane (London: SCM Press, 1966), p. 311.

[26] *The Barmen Declaration*, 1, Cochrane, p. 334.

is to exclude, logically. But if they were once true, they are always true, even though we may need to explain, gloss and expand them in all kinds of ways.

Yet those confessions are not 'static' in the sense of being timeless principles written in stone. (There is reason to suspect that fears of Platonism underlie many expressions of suspicion of propositionalism.) Indeed, it is conceivable that some of them may come to be rejected or ignored, though I hope and expect not. The point is that they are not being placed as un- questionable authorities before which we must bow – unless, of course, they are true, in which case we have no choice, any more than we have choice about what will happen if we try to breathe under water. They are *confessions made in response to revelation, and so become, or may become, mediators of it.* The making of confessions began early in the church, and is continuous with the practice of ancient Israel. Paul's writings, we are told, from soon after the death and resurrection of Jesus, contain numerous confessions which are almost certainly citations of words predating him. Certainly, he is explicit that some of his teaching comes directly from his teachers. Of the making of confessions, there is, it seems, no end, and there is certainly no breach in the process, though, alas, for far too much of the church's history they have taken the form of legal enactments. (That is another reason why we have come to be distrustful of them.)

In early times these confessions came together in what Irenaeus called the rule of faith (or, significantly, the rule of truth).[27] He was here building upon something that clearly has its roots in the New Testament, as we shall see in a later lecture, particularly in the light of C. H. Dodd's contention that there appears to be a common, though not rigidly uniform, structure to the early proclamations of the faith. But let us concentrate for now on Irenaeus, who uses the rule of faith in his argument with the Gnostics. So far as the doctrine of creation is concerned, the rule teaches that 'there is one God Almighty, who made all things by his Word, and fashioned and formed, out of that which had no existence, all things which exist'. The point to be realised is that Irenaeus exercises

[27] Irenaeus, *Against the Heresies*, I 22.1.

considerable freedom and flexibility in developing what he had received and in directing it against the heresies of the Gnostics. He cannot deny its basic thrust, because that would turn the faith into something different – and that in its turn is because it is a revealed religion – but is by no means tied to unchanging forms. Indeed, he is one of the great innovators in theology, particularly as one of the originators of the doctrine of creation out of nothing.[28] There are, to be sure, variations within the credal confessions of the Christian church, some of them of major import, like the difference over the *Filioque*, which continues to be at the root of the division of East and West. There is also reason to hold that to appeal to the so-called Vincentian canon is to cry for the moon, for there is probably no way of employing it with integrity. But, despite all the blurred boundaries, there is something recognisably the Christian faith, and it is transmitted in a range of credal forms which for all their variations, for all their requirement of the exercise of theological judgement and discussion, are fundamentally *stable*.[29] Another way of putting the matter would be to say that there is a continuity of content and dynamic between the creed of Nicaea, the Heidelberg Catechism and the Barmen Declaration.

There is in all this no desire to make one particular form of confession timelessly final as the only form of credal mediation of the faith. The point is quite the reverse. One benefit of the Reformation and the fragmentation that is its least welcome outcome is the plurality of confessions that it has engendered. Despite the differences between Lutheran and Reformed, and despite the fact that there are contradictions between, especially, Catholic and Protestant formulations of orthodox Christianity which must be faced

[28] 'God . . . is he who, by His Word and Spirit, makes, and disposes, and governs all things, and commands things into existence' (ibid.). That latter formulation is, interestingly, in some contrast with later more modalistic expressions, for example that of the Apostles' Creed, which has nothing to say about the work of the Son and the Spirit in creation, and accordingly little on the work of the Father in redemption.

[29] Or at least would be stable, but for the rupture of tradition introduced by modernism.

and eventually resolved, it can be argued that there is an overall gain in richness from the formulating of confessions to meet particular historical circumstances and demands. But the impact of the Barmen Declaration came from its sharing of the beliefs of Nicaea, not from denying them; from its continuity with the historical parameters of the faith once for all delivered to the saints.

Christianity is a revealed religion in the sense that without the credal mediation of its contents, we should not know what it is. In what I am doing here I am emphatically not limiting or reducing revelation to that mediated through the creeds and confessions to which I have referred. There is more to say in future lectures which will, I hope, widen the matter considerably, and, indeed, widen the concept of revelation beyond the restrictive limits that theologians in the tradition of Barth and Hegel effectively place upon it.[30] I hope that it will also become apparent where my differences lie with that tradition, about which it is difficult to be precisely clear at this stage. I do not wish to deny that God historically reveals himself – in Robert Jenson's way of putting it, names and identifies himself as the Father of our Lord Jesus Christ. There is no intention to deny that God the Father reveals himself personally through his Son and Spirit. That is a conception that is not characteristically modern, as Baillie suggests, but goes back to the dawn of Christian theology. 'There is one God, who revealed himself (ὁ φανερώσας ἑαυτὸν) through Jesus Christ his Son.'[31] What is being denied is that revelation is primarily to be understood as an unmediated experience, and that is why we should draw back from some of the implications which are drawn:

> In the modern era the understanding of revelation has in many strands of Christian theology been interpreted as self-disclosure; God does not disclose something about God, but God. The author and the content of the revelation is identical. It follows

---

[30] Perhaps it would be more accurate to say that one intention of these lectures is to widen theological possibilities by *delimiting* the concept of revelation in correction of its too broad construction in some modern theologies.

[31] Ignatius, *To the Magnesians*, 8.2.

from this that revelation is not understood as a specific aspect of divine action, which could somehow be separated from other aspects of divine activity.[32]

But does it, or should it, follow that revelation is not to be understood as a specific aspect of divine action? That is, I think, the question of immediacy in another form, and it certainly relates to the often made and partly justified criticism of Barth that other doctrines are or tend to be reduced by him to revelation. We shall return to the matter of the delimitation of the concept of revelation as divine action in the final lecture.

But in the meantime, the drift of this argument should not be misunderstood. There is no intention to deny that there is a fundamental dynamic involved in revelation. Certainly, revelation does not *consist in*, as is sometimes suggested, the transmission of authoritative propositions. Rather, Christianity is a revealed religion in the sense that essential to its being what it is, is its articulation by means of affirmations and confessions in which are implicit certain claims about what is true of God, the world and human life. These confessions do not aspire to systematic completeness, but to general logical coherence. They do not aspire to watertight coherence with each other, and in some details are found to disagree, but do aspire to intellectual continuity and coherence *necessarily* with what is sometimes called the biblical revelation – an expression with which we shall have later to come to terms – and *contingently* with the earliest rule of faith and the later decisions of the ecumenical councils.

IV   *Summary and conclusion*

What has been attempted in this lecture? In the first place, the aim has been to ask questions about the systematic weighting that the doctrine of revelation receives in a number of recent theologies. There is no desire to detract in the least from the

---

[32] Christoph Schwöbel, 'Particularity, Universality and the Religions. Towards a Christian Theology of Religions', *Christian Uniqueness Reconsidered. The Myth of a Pluralistic Theology of Religions*, edited by Gavin D'Costa (New York: Orbis Books, 1990), pp. 30–46 (p. 34).

priority revelation plays in our knowledge of God, but rather to delimit such considerations from other central systematic topics, particularly perhaps soteriology. It is for proper systematic weighting and integration. It can be argued that in the theologies of Barth and Rahner, for example, the language of revelation tends to serve as a way of speaking of divine saving action, or at the very least to assimilate that action within it. The effect is to prevent adequate systematic weight from being given to divine action in salvation (or creation), so that the overall balance of a theology is disturbed. Revelation is given too prominent a role in the wrong place, so that other aspects of relationships between God and the world are crowded out and so are systematically distorted. Downing's suspicion, if not the form his reply takes, is justified. Another way of putting the matter would be to say that the tendency of theology in the modern world is to become too dominated by questions of knowing, and this leads to a consequent gnosticising tendency, or at least to a seeing of the problem too much in the light of modern developments and preconceptions. But to deny that is not to deny the importance of the epistemological dimension. There is a knowledge of the Christian faith as a kind of given, a revealed religion, however carefully controlled a function we may wish that concept to play.

Second, the importance of a theology of mediation in connection with the matter of revelation is being highlighted. Whatever it is, revelation in Christian theology is mediated. A clear example of this is its mediation through creeds and confessions. What they mediate, at least putatively, is revelation, in that they purport to be the purveyors of truths which are not invented and are expected to be believed: 'I received from the Lord what I also handed on to you' (1 Cor. 11.23). They are not, in themselves, however, revelation, whatever that is, but mediators of it; put more positively, such truths may be – indeed, are – revelatory, even if they are not revelation. But that we have not yet come far along the road will be realised by the fact that most of the terms of a concept of revelation have still to be examined. We can see their number in the analysis by Christoph Schwöbel: *A discloses in the situation B the content C for the recipient D with the result E.*[33] So far, the weight of almost all of the terms and the character of some of them remains to be decided. In that respect, the content of a theology of revelation awaits articulation. That is the point I wish to make, or at least to propagate for the sake of discussion, for this is not, yet, to essay a theology of revelation. What that will be in the end is not yet known. It will be my intention in these lectures to approach a theology of revelation by reviewing some of the aspects of mediation, and attempt to come up upon it, unawares so to speak, and catch it by surprise.

---

[33] Christoph Schwöbel, *God. Action and Revelation* (Kampen: Kok Pharos, 1992), p. 87.

Lecture 2

The authority of the other: Towards a general theology of revelation

I   *The problem*

Magna est veritas, et praevalet. The inscription, taken from one of the books of Esdras and reproduced on the base of an imposing statue of Jan Hus in the centre of Prague, was a source of encouragement to those who wished to keep alive the possibility of truth when they were in the hands of a regime living by the lie.[1] The attribution of priority, agency even, to an objective and authoritative truth has been in many times the motivating force for the overthrow of tyrants – more appropriately, it can be argued, than appeals to justice, which serve more easily as a cloak for political ambition. But the transcendence and authority of truth have come into question in the modern West, under attack as they have been from various forms of modern thought and ideology. And that brings us to the historical context of the enquiry into the possibility of a modern doctrine of revelation.

The positive force of the movement known as the Enlightenment was that it affirmed the objective and universal claims of truth and reason. If we leave on one side the fact that the way the modern era has approached the question has sometimes reeked of arrogance and self-delusion, an

---

[1] Great is the truth, and it prevails, 3 Esdr. 4.41, Vulgate.

20

overconfidence in human capabilities, we should be able to share its aim with enthusiasm. The only reason for believing a supposed teaching is that it presents itself – we might almost say, reveals itself – for one reason or another, as worthy of belief, because it is true. In this connection there is something to be said for the view, sometimes propounded on etymological grounds, of the close relation of the concepts of revelation and truth. (In Greek, both of them carry the suggestion of uncovering, unveiling.) Immediately, of course, I shall be reproached by some of those who now would throw into question the Enlightenment tradition with the charge that such appeals are 'totalising' and oppressive, suggesting that I wish to impose upon the whole human race my white, Western and male conception of rationality. But why should such charges have the appearance of plausibility? Part of the answer lies in the arrogant and self-serving ends which the great Enlightenment ideal has come to be believed to represent.

Why is this so? A major reason is to be found in the fact that the main intellectual trends of our era have replaced a concept of revelation with a concept of truth as something lying within the control of the human rational agent. In the modern world, the whole concept of revelation is essentially problematic. We appear to be required to make a choice between revelation and autonomous reason. Because it is believed that revelation takes away our autonomy and leaves us in thrall to the authority of others or of the impersonal other, it becomes necessary to replace it with pure un-trammelled reason. On the other hand, if reason is autonomous and self-sufficient, we do not need revelation. We need only to find things out for ourselves. This, it appears, is the price of our adulthood, of having the maturity to use our own minds, of having the courage to be wise. One leading authority for such a claim – and the word authority is being used deliberately, to express something of the irony of the situation – is that of Kant, whose disciple, the young Fichte, built upon the foundations of the master a critique of all revelation. In it, he is not far from saying that the only revelation we can accept as being from God is one that we already know to be true on the grounds of autonomous reason.[2]

Are we bound to choose between discovery and revelation, between autonomy and authority? Making the matter an absolute choice is an absurdity, and in this lecture an argument will be developed to show that revelation, in a number of senses, is integral to our being in the world. Not only that, but it will be developed by building upon one of the themes of the previous lecture, that revelation is in large measure something that is mediated to us, by and through the other. We require the other if we are to know anything at all; we therefore require revelation if we are to understand our neighbour and the world, even leaving God out of the discussion for the moment. Another way of putting the matter would be to return to the theme of the opening paragraph, that an objective truth, standing over against us, is not alienating but salutary: 'all Truth,' said Coleridge, 'is a species of Revelation'.[3] If he is right, there is a necessary relation between being true and being revealed. Only some of the implications of so momentous a claim can be explored in one brief lecture, and I shall therefore concentrate on the way in which people and things reveal aspects of their truth to us.

II *Personal revelation*

The first of the examples to be used is the easiest, the later ones perhaps of greater theological significance with respect to the current crisis of revelation. We begin, then, with the matter of the revelation of one person to another. When J. G. Hamann enunciated the revealing paradox, 'Speak that I may see thee',[4] he opened a window on the mystery of personal revelation. We do not truly know the other unless he or she opens him- or herself to be known. Knowledge of the other is

---

[2] J. G. Fichte, *Attempt at a Critique of all Revelation*, translated by Garrett Green (Cambridge: Cambridge University Press, 1978), for example p. 134.

[3] Samuel Taylor Coleridge, *Collected Letters of Samuel Taylor Coleridge, Volume II. 1801–1806*, edited by E. L. Griggs, (Oxford: Clarendon Press, 1956), p. 388.

[4] Cited by Terence J. German, *Hamann on Language and Religion* (Oxford: Oxford University Press, 1981), p. 41.

mediated by all the five senses, but the saying rightly indicates word and sight as the central. What we say and how we present ourselves – for example, in the way we dress and bear ourselves – are at the centre of the way we make ourselves known to our neighbour.

In making such a claim, we must allow for one qualification, that our self-revelations are not always willed. Even if the claims of the behavioural psychologists to be able to know us better than we know ourselves are exaggerated – as in the joke of one saying to another, 'You are very well today, how am I?' – many of our self-revelations are involuntary, giving rise, for example, to evidence that could be read by human common-sense and certainly by a reliable lie-detector, supposing that such a thing could exist. The very possibility of deception, however, implies that we are able to hide ourselves as well as reveal. More important, the privacy that is so important for the well-being of the person is part of our essence, as was noted by the journalist who, commenting on the effect of the invasion of privacy, recorded the fact that birds who are continually watched pine away and die. This privacy is at the heart of the reason for the moral obliquity of brain-washing. To force people to reveal their private selves is to violate their personhood.[5] Self-revelation must be offered freely.

But to return to the main point. We know each other truly and personally in so far as we open ourselves to the other to be known. There are various ways in which this personal knowledge is mediated, chief among them forms of action in general and verbal acts in particular. Notice that the knowledge we give to each other is mediated knowledge, and not direct. Even if the eye is the window of the soul, being that place where we are most transparent to the other (and notice here Barth's pejorative definition of the bureaucrat as one who will not look you in the eye),[6] it certainly does not render

---

[5] In this respect, as James Fenton argued in *The Independent*, 15 November 1993, some forms of photography represent a breach of privacy.

[6] Karl Barth, *Church Dogmatics*, 3/2, translation edited by T. F. Torrance and G. W. Bromiley (Edinburgh: T&T Clark, 1960), p. 252.

us completely transparent. The eye too, that especially, can hide as well as reveal, and is also a form of mediation that must be read on the basis of gift.

What is emphatically not being suggested is that our knowledge of each other is by analogy from some inner entirely unmediated and private experience, as in all the arguments, initiated by Descartes, about the existence of other minds. That is for two reasons. The first is that knowledge of other persons is not simply knowledge of minds and souls, but of persons, that is to say, beings whose embodiment is essential to their being. The knowledge of the smile of the eyes or the arrogant swagger is as much revealed knowledge as that of some supposed inner character. Here the philosophies of language of Ryle and Wittgenstein can positively assist a view of the knowledge of persons as embodied and relational.[7] The second reason is that self-knowledge also has to be mediated, because here too we are beings only in relation, and cannot know ourselves without the mediation of others. Indeed, there is a sense in which for that very reason others often do know us better than we know ourselves. (It is those who are insensitive to others who are least able to know themselves.)

That, I hope, is enough to make the general case: that we know in large part as we are allowed to know, and that particularly the closer and more profound forms of personal knowledge are dependent upon willingness to open ourselves up to the other, with all the pain and risk that that involves. It means that revelation is, between finite persons, a reciprocal and conversational process. 'Our neighbours know us in our act of knowing them; and it is this reciprocal knowledge that is the kind exercised in religion.'[8] We come to know both others and ourselves as we enable ourselves to be known, as we reveal ourselves and are granted revelation in return.

[7] See Fergus Kerr, *The Later Wittgenstein and Theology* (Oxford: Blackwell, 1986), especially Chapter 8.

[8] Forsyth, *The Principle of Authority*, p. 154.

III *The revelation of nature*

Most of the foregoing is, it is to be hoped, fairly unexceptionable. When we come to the knowledge of nature, however, matters become far more contentious. Advocates of the modern view often present the scientific enterprise as the paradigm for the exercise of free human reason. Science does not depend upon authority or revelation, but upon the autonomous exercise of free enquiry. We can find a version of the dogma in Immanuel Kant. It is significant that Kant, as so often, is not so one-sided or naive as some of his disciples. He makes it clear that, on the one hand, we do have to learn from nature; in other words, that we have to accept that which is presented to us, revealed. Of course, he takes away with the left hand much of what he has given with the right, but not everything:

> Reason . . . must approach nature in order to be taught by it. It must not, however, do so in the character of a pupil who listens to everything that the teacher chooses to say, but of an appointed judge, who compels the witnesses to answer questions which he has himself formulated.[9]

We still do have to be taught by nature, even though we must rack her in our laboratories and dominate her by our concepts. If that is the case, does it not follow that science itself depends upon a kind of revelation? If we mitigate the anthropocentric and inquisitorial side of the Kantian picture, it is even more true that we must wait upon nature also. Is the world entirely passive in the laboratory, or whatever, or do we have to wait upon nature to give up her secrets? Why, in the annals of scientific discovery, are there recorded so many experiences which can only be described as experiences of 'revelation'?

That is a question which must be pursued later. But first let me show the complete untenability of the view that science is entirely the realm of autonomous reason and enquiry. Occasionally we have in our department students who come to do a degree in theology after taking one in the natural

---

[9] Immanuel Kant, *Critique of Pure Reason*, translated by Norman Kemp Smith (London: Macmillan, 1933), B xiii, p. 20.

sciences. When, in a course in the theology of creation, we introduce them to aspects of the history and philosophy of science, they are amazed. In their science courses, they were taught 'the truth'. They are not encouraged to question it, only to learn. It comes as revelation and on authority. Of course, things like that happen in theology, too. How far are some of the methods of the historical critical method, or the contents and assumptions of feminist theology, or the theology of Karl Barth, in some places taught on authority, as though they were divine revelation? We are selective in what we accept as authority and as revelation, but we all in some way or other rely on that which is conceived to impose itself upon our minds from without.[10]

Let us begin the chief enquiry with the question of how the supposed factuality of the natural world is mediated to us through the theories of scientists. Philosophical theories that science does not teach us how the world truly is remain completely unconvincing.[11] It may not be able to claim the definitive, exhaustive and infallible knowledge that was once – and not so long ago – attributed to it, and for that we can be thankful. But however provisional the articulations and rationalisations, and however stumbling the process, it seems to be beyond serious question that there is a process of unfolding taking place before our eyes, and indeed a kind of

[10] Repeated references to the topic show that the matter of authority is closely related to that of revelation. Factuality is authority. We cannot live under water, because it drowns us. To wish it otherwise is not an exercise of autonomy, but of childish petulance that things are not as we would wish them to be. How much of modern theology, especially that which is consciously modernist, is marked, if not by childish petulance, then at least by projection and wish fulfilment; and how much by a proper recognition that what was imposed in the name of truth in the past was sometimes an ideologically distorted theology which has enslaved rather than liberated? They are the two polar questions that face us in enquiring about authority. Is there a brute factuality, like the factuality of the water that drowns, that meets us in revelation, or is any appeal to revelation as authority a form of positivism, inappropriate to the way God truly is? What is the distinction between the authority of brute fact and that of the personal God? Somewhere in that distinction is to be sought the clue to such resolution as finite human minds can make of this difficult topic.

[11] On this, see Michael C. Banner, *The Justification of Science and the Rationality of Religious Belief* (Oxford: Clarendon Press, 1990).

intellectual progress. We simply know more about how the world is than did earlier generations. Our wisdom may often be less than theirs, but our knowledge is incomparably greater. Science, that is to say, is authoritative not as providing the clue to the overall meaning of our lives, as was and is sometimes thought, but as being one of the vehicles by which the truth of the natural world is revealed to us. In science we encounter the question of revelation in relation to human knowledge of the natural world.

Suppose, then, that we ask the question: In what way does the natural world reveal itself to us? and use that as the basis of asking, as was asked in the last lecture about the mediation of revealed religion through creeds and confessions, whether it is possible to come to similar conclusions about the mediation of scientific truth. How does the natural world reveal itself to us, if that is not too anthropomorphic a way of speaking?[12] There are at least two interrelated answers:

1. Through the theories of such as Isaac Newton. I choose him as an example because we are often told that Newtonianism is now invalidated by the theories that have succeeded it. There has been, it is sometimes claimed, a revolution of the kind claimed by Thomas Kuhn, a shift of conceptuality so great that a new paradigm, even a new series of paradigms, has taken over.[13] But that is untenable as a complete account. Newton's theories continue to mediate to us the motion of the planets and the behaviour of internal combustion engines, even if in some respects they have been modified by the discoveries of Clerk Maxwell and Einstein and by quantum theory. To that extent, they remain the means by which the structure of the world is made known, revealed, to us.

A parallel will indicate something of the relation of this discussion to that of the previous lecture. Might we say: the creed of Nicaea reveals to us something of the truth of Christ

---

[12] Notice the careful avoidance of anthropomorphism in the dialectic of Psalm 19: 'The heavens are telling the glory of God . . . There is no speech, nor are there words; their voice is not heard; yet their voice goes out through all the earth, and their words to the end of the world' (Ps. 19.1–4).

[13] Thomas Kuhn, *The Structure of Scientific Revolutions* (Chicago: University of Chicago Press, second edition 1970).

even though it was modified by the Definition of Chalcedon, which itself requires modification or development in the light of such later theologies, like those of John Owen and Edward Irving, which stress more the pneumatological dimensions of christology?[14] That is not, to be sure, an exact parallel, because of the differences that we must explore in later lectures deriving from the historical form that revelation of God, as distinct from revelation of nature, takes. But revelation mediated through theories is in some respects similar to revelation mediated through credal confessions. Note carefully that nothing is being claimed about the infallibility or unrevisability of either Nicaea or Newton. Simply, a parallel is being drawn. Its point can be shown by an adaptation of MacIntyre's famous parable of the fragments of scientific culture left behind after some catastrophe of destruction.[15] Suppose that much of scientific lore were destroyed, so that only fragments remained. We should no longer be able to understand and manipulate the world in the way we had once learned to do. Our knowledge of the world is mediated through the writings of scientists; if we lose those writings, those mathematisations and rationalisations, we lose the world, in so far as we are no longer able to understand and manipulate it in the way those theories made possible.

2. Knowledge of the natural world is also revealed to us through the ways in which parts of the world behave under experiment, or, to be more fashionable, through the ways the ecosystem responds to the way we treat it. There is a pattern of conversation between knower and known, differing according to the variations in each. Here we come to Michael Polanyi's insistence on the embodied character of our knowing. We do not know these things directly, in a godlike way, as the ideology of Enlightenment sometimes supposed.

---

[14] See, for example, Alan Spence, 'Inspiration and Incarnation: John Owen and the Coherence of Christology', *King's Theological Review XII* (1989), 52–5; and Colin Gunton, 'Two Dogmas Revisited: Edward Irving's Christology', *Scottish Journal of Theology* 41 (1988), 359–76.

[15] Alasdair MacIntyre, *After Virtue. A Study in Moral Theory* (London: Duckworth, 1981), pp. 1–4.

Knowledge is mediated through our senses, our limbs, and their extensions, our implements, apparatus and concepts, and only as we attend to reality through them does it disclose to us its secrets.[16] In that respect, knowledge of the natural world is similar to the knowledge of other people that was treated in the previous section. It is the outcome of our interrelatedness with things, in which questions are asked and answers sometimes mediated by or through that which is questioned, if the questions are the appropriate ones and are asked in the right way.

And, to move beyond the world of science, there is another way in which the secrets of nature are revealed to us through the mediation of human activity, and that is by human artistic endeavour. Art is manifold and various in its forms, especially if we refrain from snobbery and include crafts like pottery and weaving under its general head. Here, an exhaustive account is not being essayed, simply some insight into the way in which some forms of art can be revelatory. In the first place we can say that the shape, colour and texture of a piece of pottery can be revelatory of the way the natural world is. They reveal dimensions of our world as it really is, complementary to those revealed by science.

Similarly, in that which is called high art, we encounter examples of the way in which a great work of art can confront us, by its very otherness, with possibilities of understanding without which we shall simply not know as profoundly as we might who and what we are. Shakespeare's plays are a clear instance.[17] In discussing the difference between some of the entries for the Turner Prize and works of art of transcendent

[16] Michael Polanyi, *Personal Knowledge. Towards a Post-Critical Philosophy* (London: Routledge, second edition 1962). I believe that these examples, like those in the previous section, are further evidence for the fact that all knowledge is mediated. Is there immediate knowledge of any dimension of our world? I think not. Even music, the most immediate of our relations to the world, is not disembodied. It is heard, through our ears, and the materiality of instrument and voice, and that is the case even with the music of the spheres that opens to us something of the mystery of the creation in its deepest levels.

[17] This argument has something in common with the uses in recent theology of the concept of the 'classic'. See David Tracy, *The Analogical Imagination. Christian Theology and the Culture of Pluralism.* (London: SCM Press, 1981). I am not, however,

value, Giles Auty recently commented: 'Significant works of
art are distinguished by an extraordinary presence and reson-
ance: great vision, experience and skill – and sometimes genius
– went into their making and it is these, in essence, which they
exude.'[18] I am not at this stage concerned with the way in which
art may be revelatory in some way of the divine. What is
interesting here is the way in which the works of human hand,
imagination and mind may reveal something of the way the
world and human life are. It may be, as Victor Zuckerkandl
has claimed, that music provides a bridge between the secular
and religious worlds. But at this stage more interesting is his
view that it reveals something about the universe, and in
particular that there is more to the real world than what is felt
and seen, and that it is not in every way mechanical.[19]

IV   *The concept of revelation*

What is the point of all this for theology? It will be noted that
in the previous sections much was said about revelation, but
little about revelation of God. I was concerned with the way
in which we may speak of the world not as revealing its
creator, but itself. The interest is in the realities themselves,
and not in something beyond them. The point of the foregoing
discussion is thus to produce variations on Coleridge's dictum
that '. . . all Truth is a species of Revelation'. Why is this
important? We reach here a situation whose details will be
examined in more detail in the next lecture, but must be
adumbrated here. We are indeed ultimately concerned with
the question of divine revelation, and with questions like that
of Pannenberg, 'How can theology make the primacy of God
and his revelation in Jesus intelligible, and validate its truth
claim, in an age when all talk about God is reduced to

----

using this argument as a springboard from which to leap into the problem of
biblical authority, though clearly the Bible does sometimes have the kind of
revelatory authority being ascribed to the plays of Shakespeare.

   [18] Giles Auty, 'Down with the dustbin', *The Spectator*, 2 January 1993, 29.

   [19] Victor Zuckerkandl, *Sound and Symbol. Music and the External World*, translated
by Willard R. Trask (Princeton: Princeton University Press, 1969), pp. 367–75.

subjectivity . . . ?'.[20] But other more general considerations shape the way we approach the question. There is reason to believe that the disorder in the treatment of revelation in recent centuries, so well documented by Pannenberg, derives from a long-standing failure to make certain conceptual distinctions, and that that in turn derives from a failure of doctrine. Let me take the two topics in turn.

1. The concept of revelation. The distinction upon which so much hung in the past is that between general revelation, in reason, the created world, the soul, etc. and special revelation in the Bible and in Christ. As Pannenberg points out, the refutation of the traditional proofs of the existence of God did much damage to the concept of revelation through reason, and led to excessive emphasis being thrown on to the Bible as the source of revelation in compensation. This happened, he claims, both in the old Protestant scripture principle, which in turn fell with the criticism of its accompanying doctrine of inspiration, and in Barth, whose appeal sometimes appears to be to mere authority.[21]

That brings us to the heart of the modern offence with revelation: it is rooted in the problem of authority and the way it appears to violate human autonomy. The clue to the matter is, however, not to be found primarily in the scripture principle. If Jesus Christ is in any sense the revelation of God, then the Bible, as the sole source of our knowledge of him, is unavoidably at the heart of any doctrine of revelation. Rather, we have to seek the source of the offence in the way in which the authority of scripture has come to appear to operate merely arbitrarily. The situation is a complicated one, but has much to do with the aftermath of the breakdown of the synthesis of reason and revelation to be found in the Middle Ages before Ockham, in a different form in Calvin and again in the Protestant theology that followed. In all of those theological

---

[20] Pannenberg, *Systematic Theology Volume I*, p. 128.

[21] The charge against Barth is common enough, but overstated in view of his explicit and what might now be called postmodern reformulation of the conception of reason in theology.

eras, despite all their differences, there is some kind of marriage between reason and revelation considered as distinct sources of knowledge. The marriage was dissolved for a number of philosophical, cultural and theological reasons, but it is the outcome which has been so problematic for theology. The divorce, sometimes known as the dissolution of the mediaeval synthesis, introduced an apparent gulf between what can be called religious and secular reason, so that the two appeared to belong to quite separate worlds of thought. Religious reason, through its association with general revelation and natural theology, has come to appear a radically different kind of use of reason from that operating in the recognition and articulation of truth in general – that is, the secular, everyday revelation with which we have been concerned for most of this lecture. The result is that these forms of knowledge do not appear to depend on revelation at all.[22]

Our problem is that secular reason has for the most part felt it necessary to divorce itself from anything that is recognisably revelation. It has therefore come to appear that revelation belongs to the religious realm, autonomous rational activity to the secular. (Hence the point of Feuerbach's remark on abandoning theology for philosophy. On migrating from one faculty to the other, he claimed that he did so because he no longer wished to exercise faith, but to think.) My theological concern here, therefore, is that there can be no recovery of a doctrine of theological revelation – revelation of God – in the absence of what I would call a general theology of revelation. By that is meant a recovery of the Coleridgean doctrine that 'all Truth is a species of Revelation', and that means not only divine revelation but that revelation without which we should know nothing at all. If the features of our existence that I have outlined require us to conform our minds to the way our neighbour is or the way the world actually is, is it quite so objectionable that we should learn about God also in a similar

---

[22] Something of the point of this can be seen if we realise that Calvin was able to make positive affirmation of human achievements in law and politics. In fact, for him, the secular uses of reason were more successful than religious reason, because it is in matters of our relation with God that we are least able to see clearly, most fertile in the production of idols.

way? If we rely on the 'authority' of the other and of the world in our secular lives, is divine authority so exceptional or exceptionable? The answer to that question, as we shall see, is both yes and no.

2. This is also a question of doctrine. It is very important in this context that we do not lay the blame for the development only on godless secularisers, though no doubt they have had their parts to play. There has been a failure of theology, too, and one that we must examine in detail in the next lecture. The way in which the lines of demarcation were drawn between general and special revelation have contributed to the disorder. Perhaps some of the point will be seen if I spell out what are the main theological assumptions underlying the developments of the earlier sections. In them, an attempt has been made to show that revelation is necessary to what we call knowledge. That is what is meant by a general theology of revelation. But for the most part mention of the deity has so far been avoided. How, then, is it a theology of revelation and not, for example, simply a philosophy?

What has been said could not have been said without the tacit operation of a number of theological doctrines. One of them is the doctrine of creation. Just as Calvin said the things he did about the achievements of human politics because of his beliefs about the ubiquitous agency of God the creator, so it is here. A belief that truth about the world, ourselves and each other is attainable by the human mind cannot be held apart from other deep-seated convictions about the nature of reality. That is why the modern loss of the concept of God is part and parcel of the modern loss of the concept of truth.[23] The positive point is this: *there can be revelation because the world is so made that it may be known.* In that sense, a doctrine of divine revelation – of revelation of and by God – is supported by a doctrine of creation that holds that the created world is the kind of world within whose structures there can be revelation.

But other theological doctrines have been at work also.

---

[23] That is the burden of the argument of the first half of my *The One, the Three and the Many. God, Creation and the Culture of Modernity. The 1992 Bampton Lectures* (Cambridge: Cambridge University Press, 1993).

Underlying the claim that the natural world reveals its secrets to us, there is an anthropology and pneumatology, and they together produce further variations on the theme of mediated revelation. The fact that there is revelation of and through the other; that 'all Truth is a species of Revelation'; that there is mediation of revelation – all this requires not only a doctrine of creation, but involves us in a particular teaching about ourselves, the kind of beings we are, and about the way God the Spirit works toward and in the world. Let me take them one at a time, although they are complementary; two sides of the same coin. First, it is the case that nature does not reveal its secrets apart from structures of human rationality. In one sense, that is obvious, as we are the ones who seek to understand nature. But from the other side it is important to realise that it is through human rational activity that nature is able to be understood. That involves a belief that there is something in that human activity which actively corresponds, or may actively correspond, to the way that the world is.[24] We are able to appropriate the revealedness of nature because we are the kind of beings that we are: a part of nature, yet also such as are able to transcend and understand that of which we are a part.[25] In Irenaeus' teaching, we are the ones in whom nature becomes articulate. But that understanding is not objectivising or total, nor is it bound to be oppressive, because it is mediated through what Polanyi called our indwelling of the world. We understand the world through and in our being part of it.

But, second, this is a matter that can be understood only pneumatologically. If there is revelation of the truth of the world, it is because the Spirit of truth enables it to take place. To put it another way, the creator Spirit brings it about that human rationality is able, within the limits set to it, to encom-

[24] That is to say, there is much to be said for affirmations, like that of Francis Bacon, of the human priesthood of nature. It is thus our calling to enable the natural world to be known, in all its diversity, glory and mystery.

[25] Although the point is being put anthropologically, christology is involved in the sense that the claim of the conformity of the rationality of things with the rational structures of the human knower is undergirded by a belief that in Christ the creator all things hold together.

pass the truth of the creation. We therefore neither control nor create our knowledge, even though the concepts by which we express it are in part the free creations of our minds. Does it not then follow that all knowledge depends on disclosure or revelation? We may not as those who know transgress the bounds of what is, so that unless we listen, look and receive, we shall not know. In that respect, we are under the authority of that which is other than we, and that means the authority of the truth. That does not involve saying that all knowledge is of the same kind, but that we, being who and what we are, cannot know unless we are taught by that which is other than we, and that means by God the Spirit, albeit in diverse mediations.[26] Though nature is relatively passive under our enquiry, and though, as George Berkeley saw, we cannot attribute to impersonal nature the power to reveal – apart, that is, from the personal agency of God the Spirit – it remains true that knowledge of her comes as gift, and is therefore a species of revelation. Forsyth puts the matter well: 'the foundation of the intellectual life is itself given, revealed and authoritative, though the full significance of the revelation appears in another quarter of our being'.[27]

The allusion to Berkeley is a reminder that this great philosopher was teacher through his writings and thus predecessor of Coleridge, whose theological concern with the interrelation of knower and known echoes his. That is a very important link, for both were opponents of that mechanistic view of nature that emptied her of so much meaning, and reduced knowledge to a dry rationalism. Berkeley's argument against Locke's doctrine of impersonal and mechanistic substance is of the same form as my argument against non-revelatory views of the

---

[26] It is for this reason that I remain doubtful of the use of the concept of intuition, by, for example, T. F. Torrance, with whose theology I am often in agreement in this area. If intuition involves direct knowledge of any kind, then it may be an evasion of the mediation that is integral to a pneumatology of knowledge. But that may not be at the heart of the matter for Torrance, whose central hope is for a new conception of induction. See *Transformation and Convergence within the Frame of Knowledge. Explorations in the Interrelations of Scientific and Theological Enterprise* (Belfast: Christian Journals, 1984), pp. 113–20, and the citations from Einstein below.

[27] Forsyth, *The Principle of Authority*, p. 109.

world. This has two main contentions. First, the chief objection to all projectionist theories – that is, those that believe our acts of interpretation come from within ourselves and are not the response to something revelatory in the objective world that evokes them – is that they deny the unity and integrity of our perceptual and interpretative experience. If there is no revelation mediated from the natural world, if our 'discoveries' are not that, but simply impositions of our subjectivity, how can the manifest advances of the sciences be explained? Merely as the complexifications of our concepts, with no outside impulse or influence? If we say, for example, that the theory of relativity is *simply* the seeing of the world through a subjective focus, and tells us nothing about the world as it is in itself, would we say the same of our experience of the water that drowns us, the food that nourishes? Projectionism of all kinds breaks the continuity and consistency of our experience of things. To be idealist we must be irrationally selective.

But, second, once we concede that our acts of interpretation are in response to something that is objectively there, the question unavoidably arises of the relation between the world we perceive or experience and the concepts in which we respond. Understanding presupposes something to be understood, and therefore a form of meaning or rationality inherent within the world. From what or whom? Whence this rationality and meaning, if not imposed by our minds? Chance collocations of atoms? The answer is conceivable, plausible even,[28] but not from the point of view of the Christian faith, and particularly of its doctrine of creation. The link between revelation, meaning and some kind of personal creator cries out for acknowledgement.[29] It was Einstein who argued that the fact of our knowledge of the world is the miracle of science, that there can be, we know not how, some measure of correspondence between our words, concepts, mathematics, models,

---

[28] It is not, I believe, as plausible as the alternative I wish to suggest. Here at any rate Christianity is more consistent than its opponents.

[29] For Berkeley's arguments, see especially the first of *Three Dialogues between Hylas and Philonous, in Opposition to Sceptics and Atheists* (1713; reprinted London: Dent, 1910).

and the real world. Let us hear some of his words. 'The belief in an external world independent of the perceiving subject is the basis of all natural science.'[30] The concepts and theories by which we seek to understand this world 'are free inventions of the human intellect, which cannot be justified either by the nature of the intellect or in any other fashion *a priori*.'[31] But there is no way of grasping how this can be so, except in practice: the proof of the pudding is in the eating.

Yet it is clear that Einstein's is not a version of the pragmatism that is so fashionable in the days when there is a widespread loss of confidence in the objectivity of truth. 'In a certain sense . . . I hold it true that pure thought can grasp reality.'[32] Einstein is unable to explain the matter. One cannot, because it is, as we have already seen him say, a kind of miracle, and that is something that can be explained only by recourse to the concept of God, not as one who fills the gaps in our knowledge, but rather as the one who gives a reason why our experience of the world as a place of revelation and understanding should be as it is.

That was Berkeley's ploy: to show that our rational and perceptual experience cannot be explained by recourse to the mechanistic hypothesis. How absurd that mere impersonal mechanism – or mere chance atomic events – should account for our personal and rational experience. The only adequate account of the fact of revelation is in terms of personal agency. There are many problems in Berkeley's philosophy, and they provide some of the reasons why he was and is resolutely misunderstood. In particular, he lacks an adequate concept of the mediation of our knowledge of the world. In other words he lacks a pneumatology, for it is in the Spirit of truth that we find the reason for our being able to understand what is there. But Berkeley none the less teaches us that what I have called a general concept of revelation is absolutely necessary if we are to make sense of our rationality, our interaction with the world as knowing persons. It requires persons to speak to persons, to

[30] Albert Einstein, *The World as I See It*, translated by Alan Harris (London: John Lane the Bodley Head, 1935), p. 156.

[31] Ibid., p. 134.

[32] Ibid., p. 136.

communicate that mysterious reality we call knowledge. And that is why we cannot explain our knowledge without some recourse to the concept of revelation, and that means finally to the Spirit of truth whose action in this respect is to enable the world to be the object of our understanding.

V   *Conclusion*

In conclusion, and as a transition to the next lecture, let us return to the beginning, to the problem of autonomy and authority. As we saw, many representatives of modern culture have rejected revelation because it represents oppressive authority, against which human freedom must assert itself. But the solution of the conflict of autonomy and authority is not the denial of revelation because, as we have seen, revelation appears to be necessary for us as the kind of beings that we are and in respect of the kind of reality that the world is. Forsyth's formulation is little overstated:

> We start from the very nature of truth. It is given us. We do not make it. We have to yield to it. The laws of thought, the condition of our knowledge are not framed by us. Here we are not free, not creative. So far from being free, thought is beset before and behind by necessity laid upon it. Our mind is not a mere vitality, moving featureless like the wind; it has a formation, a destiny, which emerges in all evolution, but is not created by it.[33]

And so it is with authority. It would be possible, indeed, to claim that what has actually happened in the modern world is not that divine revelation and authority have been denied, but that they have been replaced by demonic parodies of themselves, just as in Tolkien's *The Lord of the Rings* the powers of evil are demonic transmogrifications of the good. When Revelation is denied, the revelation of the many lords and gods which stalk the earth, the principalities and powers of Marxism, fascism, the market, political correctness, come to be accepted as gospel truth. But they are parodies of the truth, and they destroy.

---

[33] Forsyth, *The Principle of Authority*, p. 108.

The question therefore is not whether revelation, but which. Granted that revelation can be mediated in an authoritarian way, and that churches have frequently mistaken their authority for the authority of God; that remains the primary objection both to some papal claims and to certain forms of biblical authority. But suppose that there can be an authoritative revelation which is also the authority of grace, to use Alec Whitehouse's fine expression.[34] That is the concept we must seek. But we cannot engage directly with this yet. In the next lecture a truly hardy perennial will present itself: how, and in what sense, are we to understand not so much a general concept of revelation as a concept of general revelation? That is to say: given that the case that the world is a revelatory kind of place has been established, is there also reason for holding that it gives us knowledge of its creator, and in what way?

---

[34] W. A. Whitehouse, *The Authority of Grace. Essays in Response to Karl Barth*, edited by Ann Loades (Edinburgh: T&T Clark, 1981), p. 142.

Lecture 3

'No other foundation'?: Revelation and the theology of nature

I *'General revelation'*

In this lecture, we shall move from what was called in the previous lecture a general theology of revelation to what is commonly known as general revelation. General revelation is the expression used to refer to that taught by Romans 1.19–20, as well as in some of the Psalms, that God's eternal power and deity is made known in the things that have been made. In traditional discussions of the topic, general revelation is often assumed to be in close relation to the concept of reason, so much so that it has determined the shape of at least one translation of the Romans passage. 'Ever since the world began his invisible attributes . . . have been visible to the eye of reason' (REB), although there is nothing in the Greek corresponding to, or, it seems, justifying, the words 'to the eye of reason'. The verse is translated on the assumption that general revelation and human reason are correlatives or even equivalents. Against this there is a case for holding, and it will be argued below, that the relation between this revelation and the faculty of reason is not as obvious as is sometimes supposed, or at least that some clarity can be achieved if the two concepts are at least considered in distinction from as well as in relation to one another.

Paul's words and those of the Psalmists teach that the creator is revealed in and by the creation. But the status and function of such revelation is the source of immense differences in the tradition, as is the implication of the passages for an understanding of human capacity to appropriate that revelation. On the one hand, discussion is linked to the question of the so-called natural theology, by which is meant that knowledge of God which is obtainable independently of revelation. But which revelation? Does not Romans 1 speak of a kind of revelation? What then is its relation to reason? That both Calvin and Barth can in different ways rightly call attention to the limits of unaided human knowledge of God, indeed to its negative value, by appealing to the context of the Pauline text – that it is preceded by a strong assertion of the wrath of God against human moral evil and succeeded by an analysis of first Gentile and then Jewish sin – shows the heart of the problem.

On the other hand, and it can be said that this is the same problem in different guise, we meet in such discussions the specific problem of the relation of the doctrines of general revelation and creation. Barth has reminded us that the doctrine of creation is as much a doctrine of the creed, is as much the product of revelation, as the other doctrines of the faith.[1] But that has not been the view of the mainstream Western tradition against the background of which we still do so much of our theological thinking. For this – that is, for the tradition of natural theology – something like a doctrine of creation is developed independently of Christian teaching about creation as it was developed by theologians like Irenaeus, for whom it was conceived in trinitarian terms. If then we are to understand the various ramifications of the question of general revelation, we must draw a distinction between a theology of nature and a natural theology. And the fact that the matter is by no means as simple as Barth may appear to have made it – that it is not simply a matter of natural theology over against a theology of revelation – is indicated by Barth's own failure to develop a theology of nature. Although he has a doctrine of creation, there is reason to suppose that he scarcely begins to do justice to the ontological question of the kind of reality that the world is, and this suggests that he, too,

[1] Barth, *Church Dogmatics* 3/1, pp. 3–22.

failed adequately to distinguish between natural theology and a theology of nature. We shall meet this problem later, but before approaching it must essay an interpretation of the history of some of the crucial developments.

II   *The God made known in creation*

As we have already seen, the question of general revelation is closely linked to the doctrine of creation, as it must be if general revelation is the revelation of God through the things that have been made, through the creation. The thesis to be argued in this section is, in summary, as follows. The roots of the modern problem are to be found in the history of the doctrine of creation and its fate in the mediaeval world. During that era, indeed, throughout the period deriving from the commanding achievement of Augustine of Hippo, the doctrine of creation came into symbiosis with a particular understanding, or related set of understandings, of reason. Reason came to be identified with a particular form of reason, and the doctrine of creation as the project of that particular conception, so that the doctrine of creation came to be couched in the conceptuality associated with a particular philosophy, or type of philosophy, so much so that it was virtually identified with it. The outcome was that the defeat of a philosophical tradition, particularly by science, came to be seen as a defeat for the doctrine of creation also. To put it portentously, the fate of Christianity in the modern world hung not on the person of Christ, but on the adoption of a particular solution to the question of the relation of Athens and Jerusalem.

We can approach an examination of the topic by asking why the discussion of universals was of such immense importance for mediaeval theology. It was far more than simply a dispute of Plato against Aristotle, conceptual realism against nominalism, because underlying the dispute were the two functions that the Platonic doctrine of forms and its Aristotelian equivalent both alike performed in the mediaeval understanding of creation. First there was the ontological function. The forms, *rationes,* etc. performed a structuring, relational, framework for the created order: they were conceived as those things which held together the particulars of our experience, their substructure. The founders of mediaeval ontology were therefore Philo and Augustine, the two theologians chiefly responsible for transferring the eternal Platonic forms from 'external' reality to the mind of God. Effectively this crowded out the trinitarian, and particularly christological, mediation of the doctrine of creation.

In contrast, the New Testament writers, if not unanimous, affirm *nemo contradicante*, that the structure – inscape – of creation is provided by the mediation of the Word through whom the world was made according to John, the Son of the parallel conception of the Letter to the Hebrews and of the Pauline expressions of the cosmic work of Christ. The Letter to the Hebrews is explicit: 'a Son . . . through whom also he created the world. He reflects the glory of God . . . upholding the universe by his word of power' (Heb. 1.2–3, cf. Jn. 1.1, 1 Cor. 8.6, Col. 1.16–17). The Philonic and Augustinian development brought it about that the co-eternal and personal mediator of God's creating work was effectively replaced by the *almost* eternal Platonic forms.

Another way of putting the matter would be to say that the Logos was crowded out by the logoi, a momentous change whose implications should be pondered. By the logoi are meant in this case the Platonic forms that became, during the crucial period in which Western theology took shape, the effective mediators of creation. While Maximus the Confessor can perhaps be understood to be moving away from the Platonic notion towards a view that the logoi represent the intrinsic rationality of created realities, it seems more likely that he continued to conceive them in a largely Platonic manner.[2] Whatever be the case with Maximus, the outcome becomes clear when they are treated as in some way eternal or semi-divine. As Augustine put it,

> the ideas are certain original and principal forms of things, i.e. reasons, fixed and unchangeable, which are not themselves

[2] 'To Maximus, the *logoi* are precisely the divine intention . . . [and] reveal the divine purpose', Lars Thunberg, *Man and the Cosmos. The Vision of St Maximus the Confessor* (New York: St Vladimir's Seminary Press, 1985), p. 134.

formed, and being thus eternal and existing always in the same
state, are contained in the Divine Intelligence. And though they
themselves neither come into being nor pass away, nevertheless,
everything which can come into being and pass away and everything which does come into being and pass away is said to be
formed in accord with these ideas.[3]

Augustine's positing of beings that are both created and
eternal shows that the contrast between the Logos and the
logoi introduces a far from merely linguistic point. It is the
theological point that Christ is displaced by the forms. The
notion of the christological mediation of creation is, as
Augustine realised in one of his rare appeals to trinitarian
thought in this connection, crucial to an understanding of
creation as both distinct from and related to its creator.[4] But
he nowhere realised the broader implications of that point, so
that the outcome, the effective redundancy of christology for
the doctrine of creation, is thus, as a number of commentators
have noted, a twofold contamination of the doctrine of
creation. On the one hand, there emerged the scarcely
consistent notion of eternally created reality, the forms in the
mind of God, a conception which endangers the unity and
transcendence of God. Harnack, perceptive as ever, saw this
clearly.[5] On the other hand, the understanding of the *whole*

---

[3] Augustine, *De Div. Quaest.* 83, 46, 2, MPL XL. 30, translation from *Saint Augustine.
Eighty-Three Different Questions* by D. L. Mosher (Washington, D.C.: Catholic University
of America Press, 1977), p. 80. We really must take extreme exception to a theology
that speaks of entities other than God which are 'stabiles atque incommutabiles . . .
formatae non sunt . . . aeternae ac semper eodem sese habentes'.

[4] Augustine, *Confessions* 12.7.

[5] 'Although Thomas rejected the pantheism of the Neoplatonic–Erigenistic
mode of thought, there are still to be found in him traces of the idea that creation
is the actualising of the divine ideas, that is, their passing into the creaturely form
of existence. Further, he holds, on the basis of the Areopagite conception of God,
that all that is has its existence "by participating in him who alone exists through
himself" . . . But both thoughts obscure the conception of creation.'; ' . . . in the
thesis of Thomas, that God necessarily conceived from eternity the *idea* of the
world, because this idea coincides with His knowledge and so also with His being,
the pancosmistic conception of God is not definitely excluded'. Adolph Harnack,
History of Dogma, Volume VI, translated by W. McGilchrist (London: Williams &
Norgate, 1899), pp. 184–5.

universe as created was thrown into doubt by the introduction within it of Neoplatonic notions of graded being. Some of the creation was truly finite and contingent, but other aspects, such as the heavenly bodies, still participated in a form of divinity and eternity. This, as Harold Nebelsick has shown, retarded the development of science in a number of ways,[6] but for our purposes the point is that the displacement of Christ by the forms or *rationes* brought about the contamination of the Christian doctrine of creation by pagan hierarchies of being, and therefore led to its effective obsolescence.

The second function performed by the Platonic–Aristotelian notions was rational and epistemological. An immediate, or near immediate, relation of the rational mind with divine rationality was posited, and its effect was to replace a doctrine of creation mediated by revelation with one directly or indirectly discovered by the human mind. The mediator of creation is not *Christus creator*; nor, as we shall see, is the mediator of *knowledge* of creation the creator Spirit. In both cases, the function is displaced to immanent realities: the continuity between human reason and God mediated by the semi-eternal (and therefore semi-divine) forms. In this way the doctrine of creation was confused with natural theology, and became almost as a whole the discovery of human reason rather than the gift of historical revelation. One effect of this was to entrench further the already well-established divorce of creation from redemption in Western theology, a connection valiantly but not altogether successfully sought by Barth in his proposal to subordinate both creation and reconciliation to covenant and election.[7] (The awareness of that is one of the moments of truth in the so-called creation spirituality.) In the terms of the trinitarian interpretation being attempted here, we can therefore add to the christological point of the previous paragraph the pneumatological one, that according to the

---

[6] Harold Nebelsick, *The Renaissance, the Reformation and the Rise of Science* (Edinburgh: T&T Clark, 1992), Chapter 1.

[7] Barth does indeed connect the two, but at the price of subordinating creation to what is essentially a soteriological, and, as it takes shape in his theology, protological rather than eschatological principle.

scheme of the mediaeval synthesis, human reason[8] effectively displaces the Holy Spirit as the mediator of the knowledge of creation.[9] In this respect, the apparent differences between Calvin and Barth on the subject of natural theology become irrelevant to the main point, that for a knowledge of God the creator both the Bible as source of revelation and the Holy Spirit as its mediator, are required.[10]

A number of commentators have pointed out the implications of this displacement, particularly as it affected the development of modern science and culture.[11] The chief problem for theology was that the late mediaeval and early modern critique of the synthesis, in which it fell apart under the weight of its own tensions, was catastrophic for Christian theology, much of whose fate was to be rejected along with the Platonic–Aristotelian world-views with which it had been so closely tied. When Plato and Aristotle were dethroned, so was Christ. But there is more. The critique of mediaeval rationality which subverted the Christianity of which it had been the support in due time brought about also the modern crisis of

---

[8] It is important here to be aware of the fact that this was human reason understood not as the Enlightenment took it but as part of a unified Christian approach to truth. 'The idea of *creation*, therefore, is the basic albeit unexplicated theological presupposition of both philosophical and revealed theology . . . ; and it underlines the ultimately theological (not philosophical) character of the whole enterprise.' Ingolf U. Dalferth, *Theology and Philosophy* (Oxford: Blackwell, 1988), p. 74.

[9] The chief weakness of those theories that concentrate attention on rational structures of a Platonic or Aristotelian kind is not only that they are limited in what they consider to be rational, but that they restrict that which may be considered revelatory. In contrast, a doctrine of creation that is trinitarianly articulated will, because it is christological, have room for the rationality and revelatory quality of material things, and, because it is pneumatological, understand the potentially revelatory quality of all aspects of the created world.

[10] The differences between the two are best characterised by the fact that for Calvin, as he frequently laments, 'not one in a hundred' realise the possibility of knowing God from his general revelation; for Barth, none can. Whether this amounts to a practical difference is scarcely worth bothering about in comparison to the major pneumatological consideration at stake.

[11] See, again, Nebelsick, *The Renaissance*, and Hans Blumenberg, *The Legitimacy of the Modern Age*, translated by R. M. Wallace (Cambridge, MA, and London: MIT Press, 1983); Michael Buckley, *At the Origins of Modern Atheism* (New Haven and London: Yale University Press, 1987).

rationality by seeking for culture a basis which was not that of the doctrine of creation.[12]

It will be instructive for our purpose to trace some episodes in the complex and many-sided developments which brought things to their present pass. The destruction of the synthesis can be seen especially in the teaching of Ockham that the forms do not exist even for God. The effective abolition of metaphysics by Ockham and its replacement by an appeal to authoritative revelation may appear to support the argument that the doctrine of creation should be moved from the realm of natural theology to the corpus of revealed theology. But for a number of reasons this will not be the contention here. First, because it subverted the rationality of theology, thus severing *any* link between revelation and reason, Ockham's revolution in practice achieved the opposite of what is required. It destroyed the old link, but had nothing to put in its place but mere authority. The reason why this is unsatisfactory lies in the fact that the doctrine of creation should be understood not simply as the *product* of revelation – that is to say, in terms of its origins; but also – in terms of its *function* – as the basis for the universal rationality that theology and modern culture alike so desperately require. Any merely voluntarist and authoritative theology of revelation must therefore be avoided if our concern is with a proper understanding of the relation between revelation and reason. As things turned out, the destruction of the Platonic–Aristotelian framework was in the long run also the destruction of the rationality of theology and of the unity of Western culture.

The second point shows why this is so. The evidence suggests that Ockham's nominalist theology served finally to subvert rather than to establish the doctrine of creation, because it displaced the centre of meaning and truth from the divine to the human creator. In that respect, Ockham is the source not

[12] Here it is worth alluding to the brilliance of Hegel's insight that in the doctrine of the Trinity is to be found the clue to the unity of things. The weakness of his thesis is that by making human reason the locus of divine revelation he simply reproduced the problem. Revelation is again replaced by reason, and it is no accident that there are echoes both of Neoplatonic emanationism and an Aristotelian self-thinking God in his recasting of Christianity.

the solution of the worst of the problems of modernity. This is well illustrated by the thesis of Hans Blumenberg that modernity arises when the basis of rationality is displaced from divine to human agency.[13] The arbitrary will of the Ockhamist deity comes to be metamorphosed into the arbitrary will of the human agent. Blumenberg welcomes the development but it can be argued against him that it is the root of the current irrationalism and fragmentation that bears the name of postmodernism. If each individual human being is a separate source of rationality, then the collapse of all communication and community can only be around the corner. (At least it would be but for the residual common sense that will prevent people from swallowing the more absurd flights of postmodern dogma.)[14]

It is this connection that some reference should be made to one of the long-term effects of the Ockhamist displacement, foundationalism and the various contenders for its crown. What is foundationalism? Broadly speaking, it is the belief that there must be universal and common epistemic foundations for anything claiming to be thought, or authentically 'scientific', foundations moreover which are determinable in advance of any particular object of enquiry.[15] The foundationalism that is so much in dispute today is that which belongs to what Alasdair MacIntyre, after Habermas, labelled the Enlightenment project.[16] It has taken two forms, the pure rationalist, which, in the formulation descending from Descartes, requires that all claims for truth base themselves on universally agreed conceptual foundations, and the empirical-rationalist, descending from Locke, which replaces the pure concepts of the Cartesian doctrine with the

[13] Blumenberg, *The Legitimacy of the Modern Age*, pp. 219–20.

[14] See Christopher Norris, *Uncritical Theory. Postmodernism, Intellectuals and the Gulf War* (London: Lawrence & Wishart, 1992).

[15] I am grateful to Alan Torrance for suggesting improvements to the even sketchier definition contained in an earlier draft of this chapter. I have discussed the matter in more detail in 'Universal and Particular in Atonement Theology', *Religious Studies* 28 (1992), 453–66 and *The One, the Three and the Many*, pp. 129–35.

[16] MacIntyre, *After Virtue*, Chapter 5.

incorrigible data of experience. The best known recent discussion of foundationalism in relation to the doctrine of revelation is that of Ronald Thiemann, who, in *Revelation and Theology* accuses of it three representative modern theologians. By foundationalism he means an attempt to base revelation on intuited foundations which are in some respect foreign – extrinsic – to that which they seek to base.[17]

His alternative, as is again too well known to require rehearsal, is to appeal to a form of narrative theology, in which God is co-given with the narrative in such a way that an external foundation is not required. In the first chapter I suggested some reasons why this approach is inadequate. A further one can now be offered, although it is not a new one. To base a theology in narrative, that is to say, to turn the narrative into the revelation, appears to preclude any discussion of the grounds for preferring one narrative to another, whether in question are rival versions of the Christian narrative, and they will, of course, be various, especially under modern conditions, or the narratives told by different religions. That may appear to be a recipe for tolerance. If all that I can claim is to have what seems to me to be a better narrative than, say, the Buddhist's, am I not bound to live in peace with my partners in conversation? But the question makes a false assumption, that relativism leads to peace. It does not, because not only does it evade the prior – logically prior – question of whether and in what sense what we say is true, but also increases the likelihood of violent conflict. If we in effect abandon any appeal to universal and common standards of humanity and rationality on the basis of which we may communicate and discuss our differences with our neighbour, a dialogue of the deaf is more likely to eventuate.

The dispute about foundationalism is therefore more than a merely intellectual or 'academic' dispute, for it brings into the centre the question of the basis of our common human life on earth and the institutions which form the framework

---

[17] Ronald Thiemann, *Revelation and Theology. The Gospel as Narrated Promise* (Notre Dame: University of Notre Dame Press, 1985). The guilty men are Locke, Schleiermacher and T. F. Torrance.

for that life. It is for that reason that the Enlightenment's commitment to universal and objective truth is much to be preferred to the fragmented world of postmodernism, in which there is no reason why we should bother to speak to each other expecting to be understood. What, then, is wrong with foundationalism? It is not that it seeks a common basis for rationality, but that it seeks the wrong one and in the wrong way. It seeks the wrong basis, because it seeks one that is merely secular:[18] something inherent within human reason and experience. It thus expects human reason to ground itself. It seeks it in the wrong way, because it believes that it can find what it wants apart from revelation. Another way of putting the matter would be to say that it is intellectually Pelagian, believing that something eternally and universally true can be founded on human rational and scientific effort alone. Thus Ronald Thiemann is right in one of the points on which he insists in his book: that grace – prevenient grace – is the basis of the doctrine of revelation.[19] That, at least, is encouraging support for one of the central concerns of these lectures: to put the doctrine of revelation in its systematic place, in relative subordination to other doctrines, so that the part may not become the whole, and thus strengthen rather than weaken its position.

But that consideration only opens up a further question, one only alluded to in Thiemann's treatment. How far does a narratively identified gracious action provide sufficient weight to achieve what is required of it? We cannot in a discussion such as this avoid the question of ontology, the question of

[18] Whether Descartes' foundation in the innate ideas can rightly be described as secular is, to be sure, doubtful. But there is a secularising direction, in that the source of revelation is to be found in himself, in the contents of his mind as it now is, that is, as essentially unfallen and thus understood rather differently from the account in Romans 1. Augustine's *rationes aeternae* are transferred from the divine to the human mind. The essential inadequacy of Descartes' position was recognised by Kant, whose solution only served to exacerbate the problem. As the arch modern foundationalist, Kant attempted to found scientific culture in the timeless structures of the cognising mind, an enterprise that Hegel in turn soon claimed to be viciously foundationalist and procrustean, only himself to found a more radical form of foundationalist idealism.

[19] Thiemann, *Revelation and Theology*, Chapter 5.

who and what kind of being is the God supposedly made known
in narratively characterised action. If we are to approach an
answer to the question of why we are to adopt one narrative
rather than another, we cannot be content with a deity merely
economically identified, a God merely known in narrative,
revelation and the rest. The reason is this. The concept of
God is intrinsically universal. It is not simply a question of
juxtaposing various narratives in which God is allegedly
identified, because of the inherently imperialistic connotations
of the concept with which we are dealing. However else we
may also wish to understand the idea of God, we cannot, I
believe, evade the fundamental implications of the concept
of God as the one who is the source of all being, meaning
and truth. Therefore, all claims for truth in some way or other
have their basis in him. That is why the denial of the concept
of objective truth – however that objectivity be understood –
is tantamount to a denial of belief in God, as some
postmodernists have realised. To invert Dostoyevsky's famous
saying, if everything is permitted, then there is no God. The
obverse also follows, that the affirmation of the existence of
God generates a concept of objective truth, so that those
who believe in God are bound – theologically bound – to face
up to the questions of the conflict of claims and the criteria
for choosing one alleged truth rather than another. If my
story differs from yours at a fundamental level, then at least
one of us has things wrong.

At one level, that is a matter of logic, that A and not-A
cannot both be true: either Jesus is the saviour of the world, or
he is not; and if he is, then others cannot be, or at least cannot
be so in the same sense. But the fact that some do not accept
the apparent claims of logic in this matter, and become for
various reasons radical relativists, for example, shows that far
deeper matters than logic, important though that is, are at
stake. To approach the chief one, let me ask a number of
questions which, though not merely rhetorical, are probably
unanswerable, at least in a direct sense. Why did the Enlightenment quest for a merely secular theory of universal meaning
and truth generate the doomed project now known as
foundationalism? Why has the failure of that quest in turn

convinced so many, against the apparent requirements of logic, that there is no truth, only a series of finally solipsistic expressions of opinion?

An answer can be approached with the help of a recent attack on postmodernism. Commenting on Baudrillard's claim that the Gulf War did not happen, Christopher Norris comments: 'it is Baudrillard's contention that we now inhabit a realm of purely fictive or illusory appearances; that truth has gone the way of enlightened reason and suchlike obsolete ideas; that "reality" is nowadays defined through and through by the play of multiplied "simulacra" or reality-effects . . . .'.[20] Norris has his own quite proper political reasons for mounting the attack that he does on such absurd notions. But there is another lesson to be drawn, and it is that the failure is essentially a theological one whose centre is to be found in the doctrine of creation, especially with regard to its implications for a theology of nature, and the implications of that in turn for an under-standing of what might be meant by universal rationality. To these we now turn, and, interestingly, to a theologian who was in some ways a forerunner of the late mediaeval who has served in this section to embody the problems of modern developments.

III   *The christological factor*

It is in two features of the thought of Duns Scotus in which, albeit sketchily, he returns to aspects of a trinitarian theology of creation that the promise of more satisfactory developments is to be sought. The first is his doctrine of the univocity of the concept of being. What does this mean? Simply, that there are not degrees of being, but things just are. To say that God is and to say that the world is are not two different kinds of judgement, even though they concern distinctly the infinite and finite realms. There is good reason to believe that this is a peculiarly Christian teaching, at once the fruit of revelation and, as Harold Nebelsick has recently argued, one of the doctrines whose recovery made modern science possible. In

---

[20] Norris, *Uncritical Theory*, p. 14.

what sense is it the fruit of revelation? It is a peculiarly Christian theological insight that there are not degrees of being, but a duality. There is God, and there is creation. Robert Jenson some time ago indicated the general character of the innovation in ontology which trinitarian thought made possible:

> The ontology of late antiquity had as its key operating principle the idea of degrees of being, the idea that there are sorts of entities distinguished from each other by being more or less real, by reflecting God's nature at fewer or more removes . . . Gregory [of Nyssa] denies the whole principle. So far as 'being' is concerned, a thing either is or is not, and that is all . . .
>
> Eunomius shows how he can speak of degrees of being, when he calls 'being' a 'value-predicate' . . . Gregory is indignant at the notion that being is a value. 'Whoever thought of such a thing?' he asks. Now of course the entire ancient world thought just such a thing . . .
>
> Thus the whole ontological scheme is redone by Gregory. There are no degrees of being. There are simply different sorts of being, distinguished not by degree but simply by difference.[21]

As has already been suggested, it is in its relation to the growth of modern science that the development has made its greatest impact. Modern science could not develop until the defeat of the doctrine that the heavenly bodies were of a different substance from the earthly. Aristotelianism taught that they were eternal, and therefore belonged on a hierarchy of being. Nebelsick points out that Philoponos as early as the sixth century had taught that:

> the cosmos as a whole was composed of the *same kind of matter* and was subject to the *same laws*. Hence, in direct opposition to prevailing thought, he both rejected the dichotomy between the *finite earthly* and the *infinite eternal* heavenly realms and recognised the importance of earthly reality.

[21] Robert W. Jenson, *God After God. The God of the Past and the God of the Future, Seen in the Work of Karl Barth* (Indianapolis and New York: Bobbs Merrill, 1969), p. 120.

> Further, Philoponos . . . insisted that nature could not be understood as the finite representation of infinite reality but as real in itself.[22]

Here we return to the problem of natural theology, indeed to its heart. If nature is to be understood no longer as the finite representation of infinite reality, but in *secular* terms, in its own right, in what sense can it be said to be revelatory of God? How shall we be able to say with Paul that God's eternal power and deity is revealed in the things that have been made? Do we not once again lose the theology of creation along with the loss of Aristotle? Some treatment of that question will be attempted below.

But, before that, we come to the second of Scotus' contributions, and the one most tantalising in its formulation, and it is to be found in his famous disagreement with Thomas Aquinas over christology. As is well known, Scotus, in disagreement with Aquinas, taught that there would have been an incarnation even if Adam had not fallen. One of the reasons Aquinas gives for denying the speculation that the incarnation would have happened even if there had been no sin is that creation is naturally ordered to God.[23] Because he had Aristotle, Aquinas did not need a christological mediation of the doctrine of creation. Scotus' opposing view that Christ is definitive for the relation of God to the whole world at least opens up the possibility of a return to a christological mediation of creation, as both T. F. Torrance[24] and Nebelsick have suggested. And this returns us to the claim with which I am

---

[22] Nebelsick, *The Renaissance*, p. 13. It is not being suggested that the development of science was achieved by theoretical influences alone. That Galileo looked through a telescope and saw something of the nature of the heavenly bodies is also a relevant factor, though the fact remains that something drove him to do so. The claim is that particular intellectual developments were a necessary, not sufficient, reason for what took place.

[23] Thomas Aquinas, *Summa Theologiae* 3a. 1, 3, ad. 2. Ad perfectionem etiam universi sufficit quod naturali modo creatura ordinetur sic in Deum sicut in finem. In this essentially unitarian mode of thought, it does not seem to have occurred that the creature might be 'naturally' ordained to God *through Christ.*

[24] T. F. Torrance, *The Hermeneutics of John Calvin* (Edinburgh: Scottish Academic Press, 1988).

concerned. The doctrine of creation is the fruit of revelation, biblical and christological revelation, indeed. Without
it, the ontological discoveries which we have found in
Gregory of Nyssa, Philoponos and other early theologians
simply could not have been made. What it helped to achieve
in the late mediaeval and modern development of their
insights is the destruction of the *logical* link between the
doctrine of creation and natural theology.[25] The conclusion
is inescapable: general revelation and natural theology are
two quite distinct categories, and should not therefore be
confused. God may be revealed in the things that have been
made, but it does not follow that the discernment of this
truth is achievable by unaided reason alone. Our knowledge of general revelation is the fruit of the gospel,
christologically centred as that is. Without that, we do not
see the world for what it truly is. Perhaps it was because he
was feeling for that theology that Scotus was able to develop
the ontological insights that he achieved.

What is the point of all this? The doctrine of creation is that
which provides a common foundation for all the human
enterprises we call culture, not just theology but science,
politics, ethics and art as well. In the high Middle Ages the
foundation was provided by theology, but not by a theology of
revelation. More specifically, it can be said that the framework
for culture was provided more by Aristotelian–Platonic
formalities than by a theology of creation. It is arguable that
one of the reasons for the rejection by Scotus and Ockham of
their philosophical past was that they rejected the enterprise
of basing Christian thought on a pagan philosophy.[26] The
outcome was, as we have seen, on the one hand, the rise of the
dominating aspect of modern culture we call science, with its

[25] Though the link lived on in the philosophy of mechanism, the fact that that
was even more disastrous for theology can only lead us to be grateful for the
requirement that we now think things out anew.

[26] Efrem Bettoni, *Duns Scotus. The Basic Principles of his Philosophy* , translated by
B. Bonansea (Westport, Connecticut: Greenwood Press, 1978), p. 154, puts Scotus'
relation to the Scholastic tradition far more politely ('Scotus is not completely
satisfied'), but makes the point that he was dissatisfied with the divine mind's passivity
towards the *rationes aeternae.* He cites the *Op. Oxon.* I.35, q. unica n. 5: 'This seems to

immense benefits and threats; and on the other the rise of those aspects of culture which set themselves in direct opposition to revealed Christianity. That schizophrenic development underlies the apparent fragmentation, even dissolution, that threatens late modern culture. In the remainder of the lecture two major dimensions of the question raised by the historical development will be explored.

The first concerns what can generally be called a theology of nature: an account of what things naturally are, by virtue of their createdness. In the Middle Ages this was generally provided, as we have seen, by what we can call the Platonic–Aristotelian synthesis. In the modern West, it was provided by what is now called foundationalism, the common foundations supposedly provided by reason and science. But foundationalism, as we are so often reminded, is mortally wounded, and with its loss – and it is scarcely possible to exaggerate the effect – we lose the common framework within which our culture was ordered and our moral difficulties approached. Like the mediaeval, the modern enterprise has collapsed, or is collapsing, under the weight of its own inadequacies. That is the truth in anti-foundationalism. But its danger is the loss of any framework for the ordering of culture and thus in the fragmentation that engenders so much anxiety in modern thought.

The aspect of the doctrine of creation which concerns us here is accordingly its function in the establishment of universal structures of meaning. The ontological function of the doctrine is to teach that the world is made in such a way that there is an at least potential correspondence between the way that it is and the way in which human reason and culture may come to be. Positively, it can be argued that science as an enterprise of discovery is grounded in the doctrine of creation, and it indeed appears to be the case that without it what we call science would

---

vilify the divine intellect, which in this case becomes passive in regard to the objects known through these *rationes*. The knowledge of these *rationes* on the part of the divine intellect would be determined by the presence of the objects.' That is the crucial objection to Augustine's ontologically hybrid concoctions.

not have come to be. Negatively, we can say that certain possibilities are ruled out by the doctrine: for example, the hypothesis entertained in some science fiction that there might appear in our experience beings so alien that they are completely unintelligible.[27] The world is diverse, but not that diverse. It has the same structures of being and rationality everywhere. They can be misused, distorted and the source of immense evils, as preachers of ecological doom are making all too apparent. But they are still there. 'Laws which never shall be broken / for their guidance he has made.' There is something to be said even for that rather deistic (foundationalist?) hymn.

But let us develop rather the positive side of things, the one revealed by modern science. Science could not come to be until it came to be believed that the structures of material reality, the world presented to the mind through the senses, were intelligible in their contingent relations. There is much to be said for the view, though other doctrines deriving from the Enlightenment continue to die hard, that that is the inescapable discovery of recent historical and conceptual studies. Without the doctrine of creation out of nothing which affirmed the rationality, contingency and non-divinity of the material world, the rational and experimental techniques which have brought such immense enrichment of human culture simply would not have been.[28] It follows that apart from revelation, biblical revelation, that would not have taken place. The doctrine of creation out of nothing, which teaches both the sheer freedom of God in creation as well as the distinction between God and everything that is created, does not appear to have been propounded outside those whose thinking was shaped by the biblical tradition. 'Things happened thus and therefore thus they must have happened.'[29] Everywhere else

[27] Underlying this point is one I owe to Stephen May, that science fiction is essentially the product of a culture that has abandoned belief in God.

[28] See especially Michael Foster, 'The Christian Doctrine of Creation and the Rise of Modern Natural Science', *Mind* 43 (1934), 446–68, reprinted in C. A. Russell, ed., *Science and Religious Belief. A Selection of Recent Historical Studies* (London: Open University, 1973), pp. 294–315.

[29] R. Hooykaas, *Religion and the Rise of Modern Science* (Edinburgh: Scottish Academic Press, 1972), p. 162.

the eternity of at least aspects of the universe have been taught, and what is eternal is at least potentially divine, and so not the subject for experimental science.

That leads into an apparent circle. The doctrine of revelation – the general concept of revelation explored in the previous lecture – depends upon the doctrine of creation, for it is an implication of that doctrine's affirmation of the reality and meaningfulness, both in itself and to the human mind, of the world as God's world. Yet the doctrine of creation is itself the product of revelation for, according to the logic of these lectures, without revelation we should not have a doctrine of creation. Is the circle a vicious one? Not if one important point is made. In making it, we can share the concerns of the intratextualists and postmoderns who claim that we are unable to gain an absolute and objective transcendent perspective upon our world, but are *in certain respects* limited to our historical and conceptual situation. The solution is to realise that the two doctrines, of creation and revelation, are to be understood at different levels. The doctrine of creation is a material teaching, which, if we are orthodox Christians, we have come to hold, not irrationally, but not on the basis of autonomous reason either. By contrast, the doctrine of revelation tells us where the belief in creation has come from: that is to say, it gives some reasons for holding beliefs that cannot be discovered by ourselves. That is the whole point of a doctrine of revelation, which is what it is precisely by virtue of the fact that by revelation we are taught what otherwise we could not know.[30] It is therefore a second order doctrine, in contradiction of the recent tendency – for example, in Barth – to make revelation, or its equivalent, a first order doctrine, and to relegate the material doctrines, like those of Nicaea, to being second order.[31] The doctrine of revelation tells us that we

---

[30] Thus the doctrine should not be used, as Thiemann has rightly argued, to cross an otherwise unbridgeable epistemological gap (*Revelation and Theology*, pp. 43, 48). Rather, its employment presupposes that a gap has already been bridged, so that the justification of revelation, such as it is, can be made only *a posteriori*. Whether Thiemann would be convinced by this account is another question.

[31] I am here in fundamental disagreement with Lindbeck, *The Nature of Doctrine*, e.g. p. 94. Enlightenment-led discussions of the nature of doctrine – that is to say, discussions which make epistemology the material centre, even if

cannot discover certain things unless we are taught them. That is the point of the argument of the previous lecture, that all kinds of disciplines and enterprises depend upon revelation, so that we may say, against Kant, that it is as important in science to be taught by nature as to constrain nature to our methods. The same follows, allowance being made for differences, with the revelation of God in Christian theology.

The outcome of the argument so far as the material content of theology is concerned is that there is an immense difference between a theology of nature and a natural theology. A theology of nature is the gift of biblical revelation, for it teaches us that the unity of things is upheld neither by the formal causality of the Greeks nor by the supposed omnipotence of human reason, but by the incarnate Lord whose work on earth was achieved in the power of the Spirit and in weakness. It follows that it is because we have a theology of creation derived from revelation – that is, biblically mediated revelation – that we can seek for the glory of God in the things that have been made. That this is not mere theorising, but has practical import can be illustrated from a recent book on the theology and science of Michael Faraday. In it Geoffrey Cantor shows that it was Faraday's biblicism that drove his science. Particularly relevant was his belief in the authority of the Book of Genesis:

> Faraday conceived the laws of physics and chemistry as willed by God at the Creation. Moreover, the world manifests the aim

---

they want to deny 'epistemology' – make discussions of method primary, those of content secondary. But what is this except to repeat the Kantian and foundationalist error that epistemology is prior to the practice of a discipline? Recall Barth's report of Hegel's anti-Kantianism: 'It was in him to ridicule the demand for a theory of knowledge by saying that there was as much sense in it as the demand of the Gascon who did not want to go into the water before he could swim. The interests of the theory of knowledge, he said, were best served in the act of a truly rational knowledge.' Karl Barth, *Protestant Theology in the Nineteenth Century: Its Background and History*, translated by B. Cozens and J. Bowden (London: SCM Press, 1972), p. 393. Needless to say, one cannot accuse Barth, as one can Lindbeck, of relegating material doctrines to the second order.

of its designer. Secondly, since God created a perfect system both matter and 'force' are conserved and the system is self-sustaining.[32]

But there are more subtle theological influences than that, and so we return to a variation on the christological considerations we are advancing in this section. The doctrine of the Trinity formed a matrix for Faraday's thought, for his conception of the diversity and unity of the world drew on trinitarian conceptuality:

> [W]ithin this considerable diversity the various powers are interrelated, or, as he expressed the principle . . . in 1849, there is probably *unity in one*. The clear echo of the Christian tri-unity suggests both that the individual powers are mysteriously united and also that the different powers are the outward symbols of the invisible Godhead . . . [W]hile there is great diversity in nature's appearances, this diversity is the result of a few simple laws co-operating.[33]

Here we have a theology of nature – the title of this chapter in Cantor's study – that is both derived from revelation and drove the work of a major natural scientist. Conceptions of the unity and diversity of nature derive in some way from the revelation of the unity-in-trinity of God. But where does that leave us in the quest for a concept of a revelation of God in the structures of the created world? That will be the subject of the next section.

IV   *General revelation and natural theology*

As in the previous section a distinction was drawn between a theology of nature and a natural theology, so in this one an attempt will be made to distinguish between general revelation and natural theology. The first move is to undermine further the view that the question of general revelation is the same as the question of natural theology. As Calvin argued, there can

---

[32] Geoffrey Cantor, *Michael Faraday: Sandemanian and Scientist. A Study of Science and Religion in the Nineteenth Century* (London: Macmillan, 1991), p. 168.

[33] Ibid., p. 172.

be a general revelation which is ignored through human blindness and its resulting capacity for the creation of idols. The creation may reveal the glory of God, but 'scarcely one in a hundred' recognises it for what it truly is. There has, then, to be a distinction between a general revelation in nature, which is indeed there, and the human capacity to appropriate it. The need for what is called special revelation is that, for various reasons, we often do not see what is there before our eyes. We may be looking for the wrong things, or more likely the right things in the wrong way, or partially in the wrong way. That is the point of Calvin's view that without the Bible as a pair of spectacles, we are unlikely to be able to recognise even general revelation for what it is.[34] The doctrine of general revelation is not therefore something that operates in parallel with biblical revelation, but is derived from it.

Given that, in what ways might we suppose that God's eternal power and deity is revealed in the things that have been made? A number of suggestions can be made. To begin with a general point, may we not say that the world reveals the glory of God because it is creation; because, that is to say, its contingent patterns of being have their own intrinsic rationality? Another way of putting it would be that they reveal the hand of the creator because of what they are in themselves, not because they are routes to proving the existence of God?[35] On this account, the world reveals its maker not because it is continuous with God, but because it is distinct, different indeed. It reveals by its very ontological otherness. Creation is not of interest in what it means as pointing to God, but in what it means in itself, as what might be called a semiotic system. In other words, it is to be understood as a system whose intrinsic, not extrinsic rationality, is a sign of its createdness. The fact that the world is rational at all is a mark of its coming from its creator, but even that is an insight that has been attained only in cultures

[34] Calvin, *Institutes* I. vi. 1.

[35] Another way of putting this would be to say that the creation reveals the creator by virtue not of formal patterns of rationality indicating some continuity between the world and God, but of the implications of the univocity of the concept of being.

where the Bible has been a determinative influence, suggesting that it is the fruit of divine revelation.[36]

The second point is related to the first. The world reveals the being of God by virtue of its capacity to be a framework for culture; that is to say, for all the varieties of common human thought, action and art that take place within it. The fact that there can be culture is a mark of the world's createdness: 'God saw all that he had made' – both the non-human and the human creation, in interrelation – 'and behold, it was very good' (Gen. 1.31). What is being suggested is that 'secular' features of the world's being are as relevant for an understanding of the world's capacity to be the vehicle of revelation as those which are apparently religious: good art as much as, perhaps more than, 'religious' art. Those things that are discontinuous from the divine speak the power and deity of God by virtue of what they are, in themselves. The point is made by Barth's interpretation of Mozart. For him, Mozart proved that all creation praised its maker not because he was trying to prove something, to make points – that is the way of natural theology – but because he simply allowed the music to do its own work. Mozart's *revelatory* quality for Barth was that he does not try to teach but simply plays, and it is as such that he teaches us that 'creation praises its Master and is therefore perfect'.[37] The world is thus revelatory of God by virtue of the beauty, both natural and cultural, that can and does exist within it.

The third and in some ways crucial point arises from the illustration from the work of Faraday used in the previous section. It suggests that not the patterns of Platonic formality or of Aristotelian causality but trinitarian relationality offer possibilities for drawing analogies between the being of God and that of the world. The world reveals the hand that made it in the remarkable combination of unity and diversity, of relationality and particularity, that it manifests, marks that can be recognised by their analogy to the unity and diversity of the triune God.

---

[36] That assertion is not intended to deny that the Greeks achieved a belief in the rationality of things, but that they ever taught the rationality of the universe *as material*.

[37] Barth, *Church Dogmatics*, 3/3, p. 299, and Colin Gunton, 'Mozart the Theologian', Theology 94 (1991), 346–9.

Relevant here is T. F. Torrance's suggestion that we look for parallel rationalities in theology and science, in the sciences of God and of created things. The revelation of the creator is to be found in the fact that creator and creation represent parallel structures of meaning, each with its own intrinsic rationality, the one that of the creator, the other that of the created. The latter derives from the former, but 'no argument from created intelligibility, as such, can actually terminate on the Reality of God . . .'.[38] Revelation – God's personal interaction with the world through his Son and Spirit – suggests ways of seeing parallels between uncreated and created rationality, but we need not be too anxious about finding a ladder between them. God has let that down already in the incarnation of his eternal Son within the structures of worldly being.

In that sense, we do not need to be foundationalist, for the reason that there is no other foundation laid for our faith than Jesus Christ our Lord, the one in whom the creation holds together. As we have seen, that is not to evade the challenges of rationality, but to establish them on their proper basis: not on impersonal Platonic–Aristotelian structures, but the free personal relation of God to the world through his Son and Spirit. It is the trinitarian formulation of a doctrine of creation which allows God to be God, the world to be the world, distinct beings and yet personally related by personal mediation as creator and creation. Such a position, however, inevitably places much weight on scripture. Is it a weight which it can bear? That depends on what scripture is, but also takes us into the next lecture.

[38] T. F. Torrance, *The Ground and Grammar of Theology* (Belfast: Christian Journals, 1980), p. 100. In this 'viewing together' of created and uncreated intelligibility or rationality, I would not necessarily want to speak of a transformed natural theology, it seeming preferable to maintain the distinction between that and a theology of nature.

Lecture 4

'All scripture is inspired'?:
Revelation and inspiration:
the problem of scripture

I   *The spirit and the letter*

The development of the modern critical approach to scripture
is at the same time a crisis for revelation. That is almost a truism
in the light of the history of recent theology, but its very
obviousness can cause us to exaggerate the differences between
the present and the past. It should never be forgotten that
three of the exponents of the allegorical exegesis of scripture,
Philo, Origen and Augustine faced difficulties with the
historical form of the Bible's teaching which were surprisingly
similar to those of the modern critics.[1] Yet the difference
between the eras is shown in the fact that the form that the
modern development took was, unlike the ancient discussion,
in criticism of the possibility of biblical revelation rather than
in defence of a form of it. Ancient rationalism was in defence
of the inspiration of scripture, whereas its modern form is
mostly in opposition.[2] A large part of the sorry tale is that the
modern opponents of the rationalisers chose the wrong field

---

[1] Perhaps we should say unsurprisingly similar, for rationalists of all kinds find
difficulty with the concrete, imaginative form of scripture.

[2] It should be noted, however, that the defenders of some forms of doctrine of
the inspiration of scripture can themselves be rationalistic, as James Barr has
pointed out. 'The Problem of Fundamentalism Today', *Explorations in Theology 7.
The Scope and Authority of the Bible* (London: SCM Press, 1980), pp. 65–90 (p. 70).

on which to contest the matter, following that side of Origen which encouraged the search for an inspired meaning in every text of the holy book. But at least we can say in favour of the development that it produced in Samuel Taylor Coleridge one who was able to raise certain questions in such a way that he opened a route into an appropriately modern treatment of the problems.

Coleridge was acutely aware of the dilemma presented by critical study:

> If between this Word and the written letter I shall anywhere seem to find a discrepance, I will not conclude that there actually is; nor on the other hand will I fall under the condemnation of them that would *lie for God*, but seek as I may, be thankful for what I have – and wait.[3]

But he was also aware that there is in connection with revelation, and underlying the question about intellectual integrity, another important duality, between subjective appropriation and objective givenness. He realised that the question of the revelatory authority of the Bible can be answered only in the light of a careful relating of that which the Bible gives, and that in the reader which responds. That is, the problem takes the form of the perennial question of modern epistemology, the relation between subject and object. His formulation of the question is often quoted:

> And need I say that I have met everywhere [in the Bible] more or less copious sources of truth, and power, and purifying impulses; – that I have found words for my inmost thoughts, songs for my joy, utterances for my hidden griefs . . . ? In short whatever *finds* me, bears witness for itself that it has proceeded from a Holy Spirit . . .[4]

'I have found . . .'; 'that which finds me': that polarity raises the question of the relation between subject and object. And the epistemological question leads to a dogmatic, that

---

[3] Samuel Taylor Coleridge, *Confessions of an Enquiring Spirit* (1840; reprinted Philadelphia: Fortress Press, 1988), p. 26. The recommendation of waiting is, perhaps, another reminder of the essentially eschatological character of revelation.
[4] Ibid.

concerning the relation that we conceive between revelation and inspiration: between that which scripture has to tell us, and the way in which it is enabled to do it. Biblical literalism of all kinds confuses the two, and the example Coleridge gives in *Table Talk* illustrates very well the distinction which is so often ignored:

> There may be dictation without inspiration, and inspiration without dictation; they have been and continue to be grievously confounded. Balaam and his ass were the passive organs of dictation; but no one, I suppose, will venture to call either of those worthies inspired. It is my profound conviction that St. John and St. Paul were divinely inspired; but I totally disbelieve the dictation of any one word, sentence, or argument throughout their writings. Observe, there was revelation. All religion is revealed; *revealed* religion is, in my judgement, a mere pleonasm.[5]

This distinction between inspiration and revelation opens the way for a doctrine of the divine inspiration of scripture which can allow for the fully human character of its writers, and dispense with the need to wring equal meaning out of every text. We can, indeed, go further, and argue that much of the history of the doctrine of inspiration is in large measure an attempt to equate inspiration and revelation in such a way that the text in some way or other replaces or renders redundant the mediating work of the Spirit.[6]

Let us approach the problem of inspiration by mediation through a brief review of the point at issue between Karl Barth and his conservative critics. Barth is a modern theologian in

[5] Samuel Taylor Coleridge, *The Table Talk of S. T. Coleridge*, introduced by H. Morley (London: Routledge, 1884), p. 147. The problematic notion of dictation has a long history, the worst of which perhaps began at the Council of Trent: 'the Roman Church, at the Council of Trent, defined that the whole of Scripture, as well as a body of unwritten tradition, had been given *Spiritu sancto dictante*, at the dictation of the Holy Spirit', Baillie, *The Idea of Revelation*, p. 29. Coleridge's problems were chiefly presented to him by the biblicist Protestant version of the doctrine.

[6] Here I am very close to the classic Reformed distinction between the external word of scripture and the *verbum internum* of the Spirit. The modern version of the confusion of inspiration and revelation is, as I suggested in the first lecture, the tendency to turn the text, the narrative, etc. into the divine agent.

that he holds to the modern dogma of the humanity of scripture.
Where he differs from his critics is in his location or weighting
of the inspirational process. He tends to put the weight not so
much on the process by which the writers were inspired to write
what they did, as on that by which their writings by inspiration,
so to speak, *become* revelation in the here and now. The emphasis
is not on revelation *then* but on the event of revelation *now*.[7]
The charge of the critics is that this encourages an excessively
actualist view of the Bible, in effect conceding too much to the
doctrine of its humanity, too little to the intrinsic inspiredness
of the text. That will be at the heart of the question asked in this
lecture: In what sense is scripture the mediator of revelation
because of the unique inspiration of its writers? What may such
inspiration be taken to mean?

To be sure, Barth's view of the matter is in many respects
like that of the mainstream Christian tradition, including that
of Roman Catholicism, in holding clearly to the view that
scripture is not revelation, but in some sense mediator of it.
What is at issue is the nature of that mediation. Virtually
all Christian theologies posit a space between the words of
scripture and the articulation of Christian teaching. The most
conservative of evangelicals, for example, agree that scripture
has to be interpreted. One cannot, that is, read doctrine
logically off the pages. Virtually nobody holds that we are
given the word of God in an entirely unmediated sense, and
therein may lie a major difference, at least of theory, between
Christianity and Islam. It is after that that the differences begin
to appear, so that this is not merely a matter between Barth and
those more conservative than he, but of the very nature of
Christianity. At stake is the character of scripture's mediation of
revelation.

II   *The problem of historicity*

Whether we like it or not, even if we proclaim the future
orientation of Christianity and the eschatological character of

---

[7] Here is one of the places where he continues to be close to Bultmann, though
in other respects what is developed below is close to some of the things that Barth
says.

revelation until we are blue in the face, we cannot escape a
question upon which even eschatology depends: the historicity
and therefore static lodgement in time, of the basis of revelation: in a man once born and crucified, in the nation from
which he came, and in the book which claims on almost every
page, implicitly if not explicitly, to be the vehicle of revelation.
Whatever we make of the fashionable claims about textuality,
at least in this respect we are tied to the text. It is there, in our
past and present like – as someone once said of the theology
of Barth – a mountain in our back garden.

Suppose, then, that as a working hypothesis we take revelation to mean at least that which was argued in previous
lectures, the making known of that which otherwise remains
hidden or unknown. Of what revelation might we consider
scripture to be the vehicle? In recent times a number of answers
to that question have been attempted, and we might allude to
the two forms of modern quest noted by Hans Frei, for facts
ascertained by historical enquiry of the same kind as that sought
by secular methods of historiography and for timeless didactic
ideas indicated by the narratives.[8] Alternatively, we might locate
revelation in some form of existential immediacy, as appears
to be the case with Bultmann and indeed sometimes with Barth.
The inadequacies of all these approaches and others have been
related often enough, and it can be said that in different ways
they all evince a deficient pneumatology: an inadequate way
of construing revelation as mediated by God the Holy Spirit.
The work of the Spirit is in some way either replaced by human
intellectual activity, or centred in subjective human response,
on the one hand, or, on the other, made to appear objective in
a rather authoritarian manner, for example in the legal
judgement of some ecclesiastical body.

Suppose, second, that we affirm the generally revelatory
character of scripture, and ask again what is there made known
that is not knowable without the texts. We can approach an
answer by taking as a test case the first chapter of the book of

---

[8] Hans Frei, *The Eclipse of Biblical Narrative. A Study in Eighteenth and Nineteenth
Century Hermeneutics* (New Haven and London: Yale University Press, 1974), p.
103.

Genesis. The advantage of this is that it enables us to avoid crude theories of revelation, and in particular those in which the text is made to mediate supposed truths of a theologically inappropriate kind. We shall come to that question later, but it is easy to show the kinds of thing that are meant. It is wrong to seek from Genesis either the kind of philosophical structuring of reality sought by allegorists from Philo onwards or the kind of scientific facts that are sometimes alleged by certain forms of biblicism. That is to say, we must eschew any attempt to read Genesis either in the light of a philosophy or as a kind of primitive, or even timelessly valid, science. If we accept also the inadequacy of a crude mythological account which holds that we can learn from Genesis only about the structures of rationality of the primitive mind; that is, if we approach the text expecting to receive something that we should not otherwise find, then it is possible to approach an answer.

The Genesis account of creation is unique. It is not unique in every sense, for there are clear parallels between it and the creation myths of other cultures. But it is unique in presenting a pattern of divine action that is different in kind from anything else. Indications of the difference between Genesis 1 and other ancient creation texts are to be found in much recent commentary. Negatively, what Genesis 1 tells us, as is almost certainly not told by any other doctrine or myth of creation, certainly not by anything deriving from the philosophy of Greece, is that the world does not come from the body of god or gods, but is the product of free divine activity. Even if it is anachronistic to see in it an account of creation out of nothing, there is without doubt an expression of the freedom of God over against all that is other that is without parallel. In addition, a recent hermeneutical study by Francis Watson has shown that there is also to be found in this chapter a pattern of mediation that makes it interestingly and uniquely what it is, so that through it the world can be understood to be in various forms of relation to its maker.

Watson discerns a threefold pattern of mediation in the text. The first is the oft-remarked speech-act conception of creation: God speaks, and things happen. On its own, Watson believes, this creates problems, particularly in encouraging the view that we create our world through speech. Against this, he argues that 'Gen. 1 does not present the notion of creation through the word in the unified manner implied in the Johannine text. In fact the speech-act model occurs unambiguously on only three occasions in this chapter'.[9] Therefore it requires supplementation. The second model for divine action is what he calls the 'fabrication model', where the objects of creation do not immediately spring into being but have to be constructed.[10] It is not absolutely distinct from the first model, and is often, both here and in the Psalms, used in conjunction with it, and with a third, which he calls the mediation model:

> God creates immediately by command and by fabrication, but he also and simultaneously creates mediately in employing one of his creatures as the womb out of which the others proceed . . . 'Let the earth put forth . . .' . . .
>
>   The creation narrative thus makes use of three interconnected but distinct models in order to represent the act of divine creation. Each has a different role, but the full meaning of each emerges only in combination with the others.[11]

It is thus, and Watson draws out the point, incipiently trinitarian:

> This God is, first, transcendent, but the function of this concept is still to express something of the *relationship* between creator and creation, and not to postulate a deity who is so wholly other as to be incapable of creating. Second, this God is wholly involved in his creative activity, and his involvement takes the intimately bodily form of labour . . . Third, in the most intimate relation of all, this God indwells her creation, not in the form of a passive, static presence but in an active dynamic, self-transcending movement towards the emergence and reproduction of life and breath . . .[12]

Building on Watson's work I want to suggest further that in the light of the tradition of interpretation the very originality,

---

[9] Francis Watson, *Text, Church and World. Biblical Interpretation in Theological Perspective* (Edinburgh: T&T Clark, 1994), p. 140.

[10] Ibid., p. 141.

[11] Ibid., pp. 142–3.

[12] Ibid., p. 144.

and, in certain respects, offensive character of this text, have blinded exegetes to what now can be seen to be its leading message. In particular, the long tradition of allegorical and Platonising exegesis has made it very hard to come to terms with the text's celebration of the goodness of the material world; while an equally long tradition, also influenced by Platonising suspicions of materiality, found it difficult to come to terms with the claim that male and female are alike, together and as such, created in the image of God. In this respect, too, the text teaches us things that simply could not be learned elsewhere, as Calvin recognised when he taught that we cannot see the world as it truly is apart from the spectacles given us by the Bible. Or, to use another example developed from the previous lecture, it seems likely that had Michael Faraday not been what we would call a biblicist Christian, he would have been unlikely to be as critical of Newtonian mechanism as he was. Among his reasons for the rejection of Newtonian atomism and the void were considerations drawn from scripture.[13] It might be contended, then, that the text of Genesis, interpreted in the light of other aspects of the Bible, to be sure, has revelatory authority at least in the respect that it enables us to understand and articulate something of the truth of God's foundational, mediatory and redemptive relations with that which he has made.

What we gain from Genesis is thus the knowledge of a unique form of mediation.[14] We could proceed on this basis to argue

---

[13] Geoffrey Cantor, *Michael Faraday: Sandemanian and Scientist. A Study of Science and Religion in the Nineteenth Century* (London: Macmillan, 1991), pp. 190–3. Faraday was unusual though not unique in rejecting the mechanist tradition, but may have been unique in the biblical reasons he gave for doing so.

[14] If Genesis is thus conceived as revelatory, it becomes impossible to limit revelation to revelation through or in history. The latter is a way of characterising much that is expressed in scripture, but is too restrictive to cover all putative instances. And even if the hypothesis is correct that Hebrew creation theology results from reflection on history, and particularly the Exodus, the fact remains that its content cannot be called historical. Nor will the idea of revelation as God's self-revelation cover this kind of case, and therefore it too must fail as a comprehensive account. How does all this relate to the question of general revelation? Whatever else it is, Genesis 1 does not come under this either, because it *revises* our view of God's relation to nature.

that the text is therefore inspired – is the work of the Spirit – because it reveals things that are to be found nowhere else. We could support this claim in a number of ways, by comparing it with other apparently similar documents, and showing that, for example, it shows a clear rejection of the divinity of the creation, and that it has contributed to the rise of modern science. We could also insist that, along with other related parts of scripture, it provided a necessary condition for other forms of knowledge and activity to be developed. It has been a matrix for human culture as well as religion. In parallel with this we could argue that such a view is consonant with a theology of revelation that understands the Spirit to use in the process the abilities and cultural forms of the writers. Biblical revelation is thus to be understood as the making known of truths about the ways of God towards and with the created order that cannot be obtained elsewhere.[15]

How far would that take us? A long way, but not, it would seem, far enough. On the face of things, what we obtain in this way would simply be a form of theological information: facts about God and the world. Is that what we mean by revelation? Revelation certainly includes the imparting of information, but if we remain there, we are stuck with a rather intellectualist view, and the concomitant suggestion, rightly rejected by Schleiermacher, that Christian belief is the appropriation of factual information. Let us approach the same question in a different way. One of the proposals sometimes heard for the solution of the problem of biblical inspiration is that we consider the Bible as a kind of classic: a work that retains its hold as an indispensable work of literature, providing clues to our being in the world that are unavailable elsewhere. On such an account, however, we reach a similar difficulty, for there are many classics, and they give us all kinds of information – and more than that, wisdom – that cannot be found elsewhere.

---

[15] It is perhaps an implication of the doctrine of the Holy Spirit that this is necessarily a contingent matter. In theory, we might obtain the knowledge from elsewhere; in fact, we have not so obtained it. The priests of Isis in Verdi's *Aida* praise their God for creating everything out of nothing. Although this is undoubtedly owed to the writer's formation in a Christian culture, we have to concede that it is not necessarily so derived.

But they are not the Bible. We must, then, seek further for an answer to the question of the Bible's unique inspiration and mediation of revelation; not, however, an answer that takes away what we have discovered, but takes it further.

We can approach it by returning to the theme of the previous lecture, and asking what is the difference between what are rather misleadingly called general and special revelation. While scripture contains affirmations of the revelation of God the creator through his creation (Psalm 19, for example), that is not primarily what it is concerned with. We may see this if we realise that to treat Genesis 1 in isolation is to fail to see it in its own context, which is to serve also as a framework for the great story of salvation which begins with the call of Abraham. However, even that could be misleading. The call of Abraham and the subsequent story of Israel and Israel's greatest son could also be viewed as a kind of information. The unique character and authority of scripture as *revelation* is that it claims to be more than the provider of unique information, but also to be the bearer of saving knowledge, a vehicle of the word that 'is sharper than any two-edged sword, piercing to the division of soul and spirit, of joints and marrow, and discerning the thoughts and intentions of the heart' (Heb. 4.12). Knowledge of God is inextricably bound up with knowledge of ourselves.

We are, therefore, unavoidably in this context brought into the realm of christology and soteriology. The distinct mark of the revelatory character of the Bible is its relation to salvation in Christ the mediator of salvation. The revelatory uniqueness of the Bible derives from its mediation of the life of this man, and particularly his cross and resurrection, so that its distinctive problematic derives from the fact that these are past events, apparently marooned in an era to which we do not belong. But the limits of such an analysis – and of all theologies based on the supposed 'historical Jesus' – are to be seen in questions about the identity of the one who died on the cross. Who *is* Jesus Christ? is a question couched not in the past but the present tense. He is, according to the church's faith, the one who came, is ascended at the right hand of the Father and will come again at the end of the ages. If the present Jesus is the ascended Christ who sits at the right hand of the Father interceding for his people, how is he mediated – as at once and in different respects absent and present – to us? Put otherwise, if the ascended Christ is the mediator of salvation now, how is this salvation mediated? In a number of ways, we might say, but prominent among them is scripture. But, again, by what means? Does scripture *identify* only? Clearly, revelation is of the character and acts of the one who is identified, but in what way is a knowledge of them related to salvation? We can only begin to answer such a question in the rest of this lecture, but a beginning can none the less be made.

III   *Revelation and the problem of the past*

The particular quality of the Bible's mediation of revelation is derived from its mediation of salvation. It's uniqueness derives from the uniqueness of the Christ who is mediated and of that which is mediated by Christ. But this only returns us to the question with which we began concerning the relation between inspiration and revelation. In what sense, in the light of all this, is the Bible inspired in such a way that it becomes the unique vehicle of revelation? Let me try to develop a view by alluding to the picture that we usually have of the process of inspiration: of the writer sitting at a desk, with a shadowy figure over his shoulder, either actually dictating words or more vaguely providing guidance. Is this how the Spirit works? Well, why not, sometimes? Do not the artist and scientist sometimes feel that they have been given insight from beyond, like that which apparently granted Anselm his wish to find one argument with which to put beyond all doubt the existence of God?[16]

But while this may sometimes help us to understand how all truth and beauty is in some way the fruit of inspiration, it is, in our context, too individualist a picture. The work of the Spirit in this case must be understood in terms of the particular patterns of relations with which we are concerned when we

---

[16] Anselm of Canterbury, 'Preface' to *Proslogion*.

speak of the inspiration of scripture. A more adequate picture of what happens can be developed if we bear in mind two features of the characteristic work of God the Holy Spirit. In the first place, the Spirit is the one whose gift is communion, community, both with God and with the other. The Spirit is thus, among other things, the Spirit of the church. Now that is a very interesting feature in view of the fact that we are now often reminded of the truth, if it is true, that the books of the Bible are as much the work of the early Christian community as they are of individual writers. Indeed, the authors are sometimes called redactors, those who pieced together parts of the tradition into literary wholes in the light of the needs of the communities of which they were a part. Similarly, speculative biblical scholars reproduce what they hold to be the shape of the communities in and for which the books were produced. This might be taken to be the death knell of a theory of inspiration. It is not the Spirit, but the community which creates what we call scripture. But why should it be so problematic? If the Paraclete is the one who guides the community into all truth, as the Fourth Gospel promises that he is (Jn. 16.13), the Bible's inspiration may be perceived to derive from precisely this fact, that it is the book of a community, or rather of the people of God who are variously Israel and the church.

That, in itself, is not enough to establish the kind of uniqueness that I am seeking. The Jewish and Christian communities have other books which serve their lives, sometimes even the works of theologians. What is the distinction between these books, in their own way inspired, and the unique inspiration of scripture, that makes the concepts of inspiration and revelation so difficult to disentangle? Before approaching the heart of the matter, I must introduce the second of my two marks of the doctrine of the Spirit. It is that we are not here concerned with any Spirit, but with the one who through Christ brings us to God the Father. If we are to rely on the testimony of the New Testament, and particularly that of the Fourth Gospel, it is noteworthy that their emphasis is not on Jesus Christ as revealing himself, as Barth sometimes tends to suggest. It is rather on Jesus as the one who makes known, mediates indeed, God the Father. Within the complex interrelations of the persons of the Trinity, the function of the Spirit is to guide to Jesus as the one who reveals the Father. The Spirit is thus the one who points away from himself to Jesus, whose will is to do the work of the one who sends him.

The Bible's particular inspiration will therefore be found somewhere here, which means that we cannot avoid some discussion of the concept of apostolicity, of the unique position of those whose lives were bound up with him who came out of Israel and died on a cross. The apostles, and that does not mean only the twelve who are called apostles but includes the community gathered around them in the first days of the church, are those upon whom the historical Jesus, the Jesus of past history, made his particular impact as the revelation of God. Just as it is a logical truth that a proposition once true is always true, so it is a fact of our historicity that what has happened has happened, and is thus unchangeable: brute reality, although not brute reality so much as personal and redemptive givenness – what was called above, using W. A. Whitehouse's expression, the authority of grace.[17]

Part of what it means to say that scripture is inspired is accordingly to be found in an affirmation that God the Spirit enabled members of a community in a particular time to articulate what it was about that particular configuration of events that is uniquely significant for the salvation of the world. It is too external a way of putting it, as Barth tends to, to speak here of scripture as witness, evocative though his use of Grünewald's painting is, with the long bony finger of John the Baptist pointing away from himself to the crucified Christ. The weakness of the metaphor of the witness is that sometimes witnesses speak of what they see, autonomously and in their own strength, or at any rate that they are in external relation to that which they record.[18] Indeed, in one account

---

[17] See Lecture 2, note 34.

[18] There must be no suggestion that this is the case with Barth, who is somewhat more nuanced than that. What is at stake is a difference of weighting, one, however, which has important implications. According to Barth, the fact that the Bible should be understood as witness to revelation means that 'it is for us revelation by means of the words of the prophets and apostles written in the Bible, in which

of a revelatory event, the Palm Sunday demonstration (Jn. 12.16–19),.it is the witnesses who are recorded as being the very ones who misunderstand what is happening.

The metaphor of the witness suggests, or may suggest, that the work of the Spirit is to turn the human words of the writers into the words of God. The point of attempting an alternative way of putting it is twofold. It is first to express a little more adequately the fact of the work of the Spirit in ordering the community and its writings around and to the incarnate Lord, and thus of a process of formation both of the community and of its documents, in which the words are, as human, already and as a result of that process in an important sense the words of God. P. T. Forsyth put it thus: 'This interpretation of theirs, this exposition of Christ, was a providential, integral, and, we may say, polar part of the action of the total fact itself, and not a searchlight thrown on it from without.' 'The Apostles were not panes of bad glass, but crystal cups the master filled.'[19] There is thus, to use an expression I owe to Alan Torrance, an intrinsic relation between revelation and the words used to enable it to come to expression. And the communal dimension is brought out by some words of Paul: 'And we impart this in words not taught by human wisdom but taught by the Spirit, interpreting spiritual truths to those who possess the Spirit' (1 Cor. 2.13).[20] Revelation thus takes shape in an ecclesial relation between inspired teacher and inspired taught.

Second, it is necessary to say something of the advantage of the contemporary. Here we reach some most interesting

---

they are still alive for us as the immediate and direct recipients of revelation, and by which they speak to us. A real witness is not identical with that to which it witnesses, but it sets it before us.' *Church Dogmatics*, 1/2, p. 463.

[19] Forsyth, *The Principle of Authority*, pp. 131, 134. See also p. 332: 'we cannot regard New Testament theology as mainly made up of ideas which grew upon the apostles out of their personal faith, their private and tentative interpretation of their religiosity; so that they became, as "eminent Christians", the mere classics of such faith'.

[20] The reference to this text was made by Thomas Gillespie, the President of Princeton Seminary in the discussion after the lecture.

questions. Those who recognise an allusion to Kierkegaard will remember his claim that in view of the essential offence of the gospel about Jesus, the one who is contemporary with the events is in no better a position than we are as regards capacity for reception of revelation.[21] The contemporary of Jesus requires that revelation which overcomes disbelief as much as do we ('Flesh and blood has not revealed (ἀπεκάλυψέν) this to you, but my Father who is in heaven', Mt. 16.17). But there is also a sense in which the contemporary has, if not an advantage, at least a different function, and that is apostolicity. There is a particular function to be performed by those who are apostles because of their unique relation to that 'which', in the opening words of the First Letter of John, 'we have seen with our eyes, which we have looked upon and touched with our hands, concerning the word of life . . .'. Their unique and unrepeatable function is to 'proclaim also to you', but in such a way that revelation and more than revelation is mediated: 'that you may have fellowship with us; and our fellowship is with the Father and with his Son Jesus Christ'. The function of the contemporary, of the apostle, is to act as mediator of salvation to the one who is not. According to John, that was the aim of his writing his Gospel: 'these [things] are written that you may believe that Jesus is the Christ, the Son of God, and that believing you may have life in his name' (Jn. 20.31). May we not then say that the work of the Spirit in inspiration is to enable the authors to write what they have written and to enable their words to be the indispensable mediators of revelation?[22]

An analogous argument can be developed for the inspiration of the Old Testament, in the light of the concept not so much of apostolicity as of prophecy, in the widest sense of those who mediate the word of God to the present. The writers' revelatory

---

[21] Søren Kierkegaard, *Philosophical Fragments*, translated by D. F. Swenson and H. V. Hong (Princeton: Princeton University Press, 1962), Chapter 4.

[22] In what sense, then, is the Spirit to be understood as the perfecter of the text, of the work of its writers? It is not only because they record revelation, but because their words are in some way revelation. '. . . the Spirit is *in* the apostolic word, it is not simply *with* it and *in* us', Forsyth, *The Principle of Authority*, p. 141.

function also derives from their place in a community, in this case the historic community called by God to be a light to the nations and the people out of whom Jesus of Nazareth came. The question of revelation is in this case more complex, for a number of reasons, chiefly two. The first is that, although we may understand neither Jesus' identity nor his saving reality without the witness of the prophets, it is also true that Jesus' ministry represented a choice of one among the number of possibilities offered by the Old Testament for the shape of being the holy people of God. That is why, although the New Testament writers see that Jesus is the fulfilment of the Old Testament as a whole,[23] they are also free to draw upon some strands of its tradition at the expense of others and in particular those which express the vicarious suffering rather than military glory of the messiah, and the more universalistic strands of Israel's mission. The second difference in the Old Testament's revelatory character is that in Jesus, God is personally present in a way only anticipated in Israel. That is why we need not be embarrassed about the less acceptable sides of the record, for it is only to be expected that the trumpet will at times give a more uncertain sound. Choices have to be made, but they are not choices for which there are no criteria, for they are theologically informed choices. Nor does that exclude a belief that here too the Spirit works through the structures of community and the human gifts of the writers to make the Old Testament in its particular and concrete way the mediator of revelation.

IV *Conclusion and transition*

In the first lecture some remarks were made about the charge that propositions are static, and the time has now come to develop what was said there. Just as it is no discredit to have formulated something that is true, and so remains so, it is not in itself problematic that our faith is tied to a man who lived long ago and is mediated by the words of those who were uniquely bound up in historical and communal tradition and

---

[23] See Lk. 24.25–7.

in personal fellowship with him. To understand what this does and does not imply, we must draw some distinctions. The fact that revelation or its records are in one sense *fixed*[24] does not entail, first, that there can be no new divine action. It is rather to limit the scope of the doctrine of revelation against what is sometimes taken to be the implication of the theology of Barth, who appears by his conflating revelation with other forms of divine action to have given to many the – undoubtedly false – impression that because of the way in which revelation is in one respect tied to the past, there is no further divine action, only the working out of what God has done already. Biblical revelation (given, fixed, static and textual as it is) as a matter of fact may be the ground for believing that there are further divine acts to come ('Behold, I am doing a new thing', Is. 43.19), or that the ascended Christ is a living and active advocate with the Father, or that the Spirit works to perfect the creation.

Nor does it entail, second, that there is no new understanding of revelation. Again, the reverse is the case. The form of revelation is such as to encourage enquiry, in the belief that we shall learn greater things, and that the servant of the kingdom is like a scribe bringing out of his treasure things both new and old (Mt. 13.52). Must we never the less say that, short of the End – the final revelation – in Christian theology there is no new revelation, only new appropriation and understanding of revelation? According to Calvin, the Spirit enables us through the medium or mediation of scripture to see the world as God's world. Again, this is the mediation of a truth that is unchanging: though our apprehension of its content may change. That is where the discipline of theology must necessarily differ from other disciplines, which are not tied *in the same way* to past history. If God is the one who creates and redeems through Christ and the Spirit, and is made known as such by the incarnate, crucified, risen and ascended Jesus,

---

[24] That need not be to deny that the fixedness is a contingent matter: 'Could we not theoretically come across a second epistle of Paul to the Romans which the church might decide could or should be brought into the canon?' A. J. Torrance, in correspondence.

then that is the one he always is. Any new action, therefore, can be expected within the framework of this eternal revelation (or revelation of the eternal gospel). This does not imply anything about the possibility that theology may often be, and may often have been, mistaken in its interpretation of revelation, for example, in its understanding of the Trinity or of the nature of women. What it does imply is quite the reverse, the possibility of progress in theology which is grounded in revelation, and in particular the promise that the Spirit will lead the church 'into all truth'. (Here we shall not forget that by that phrase the Fourth Gospel does not mean, emphatically does not mean, into all information, but to Jesus who is the truth of God incarnate.) Therefore dogma and theology are revisable, scripture is in certain respects open to question, but revelation, mediated through scripture, is not.[25]

The third thing that biblical revelation's restriction to the past does not imply is that, because it is, in the sense we have examined, tied to past history, Jesus also is. According to the past witness of scripture, Jesus is not a person marooned in the past but one who lives forever to make intercession for us and will return at the end of the age as judge. Past revelation reveals a figure who is past, present and to come: yesterday, today and forever. The form of revelation is not identical to the form of that which it reveals, any more than the form of a scientific theory is identical with the form of the world it makes known, though in both cases there is an intrinsic relation between the two.[26] And that leads us directly into the question of the next lecture. The church today is neither historically contemporary with the apostolic community, nor yet at the end of the age in which she will know as she is known. We are tied to the past in recollection, and to the future in hope. And yet there is also a sense in which we are one with the apostolic community, and that is in respect of the fact that we are joined to them by a great chain of personal tradition. Revelation

[25] It is for reasons such as this that I believe that Lindbeck's much discussed attempt to mediate between two opposing forms of modern theology cannot succeed. Lindbeck, *The Nature of Doctrine.*

[26] Always supposing, of course, that they have things right.

may be, in one sense, tied to the past. But in another it is not, for it is mediated from one generation to another by dynamic and personal process. The next lecture will, accordingly, examine some of the questions raised by the concept of tradition.

Lecture 5

'Truth, the daughter of time'?: Revelation, church and tradition

I *Two metaphors*

The Reformation is still sometimes presented as though it was largely a dispute about the Bible and tradition as alternative sources of revelation. We have been told often enough that this is an oversimplification, and we can see the truth of this if we realise that John Calvin was in certain respects a traditionalist. This is shown by the fact that one of his charges against the radical Reformation was that its exponents ignored the tradition: we might say, took themselves so far outside the processes of history that they believed they could make it anew. In modern terms and those used in these lectures, they claimed some form of revelational immediacy: a direct relation to the scriptures without the mediation of a tradition of interpretation. Similarly, it could be said that Calvin was a traditionalist because he believed that the church had left the main road and that the Reformation was calling it back to its true course. In this respect the notion of tradition is not understood in a static or reactionary sense, but of a recalling of the church to a proper dynamic and direction, as for instance in Calvin's reassertion of the centrality of the preaching of the word and of the celebration of the two gospel sacraments.

The character of Calvin's traditionalism can be understood by showing something of how he was related to, or understood his relation to, the Christian theological past. First, there is his use of what we call authorities. Who but an exponent of ecclesiastical tradition would make such frequent appeal to the Cappadocians, Augustine and others of the Fathers? Yet, as his views of the ecumenical councils show, he was a critical traditionalist, for he would allow them only a relative authority, as compared with the absolute authority of scripture. It is important here to realise that despite the liberal use of the concept of heresy at this period of the church's life – usually to refer to some form of social, political or ecclesiastical deviance – the Reformers were not heretics in the proper sense of the word, in that along with the Roman Church they adhered to the classic creeds of Christendom. Certainly today, after centuries of critical and liberal theology, the magisterial Reformers appear irremediably traditionalist, though none the worse for that.[1]

Second, Calvin must be understood as a traditionalist in the light of his intellectual background and history. Here by tradition I refer not to acceptance of the faith that is handed on from one generation to another so much as to the way in which one stands in relation to the tradition of thought from which one emerges. T. F. Torrance has shown that Calvin emerges out of an intellectual tradition that included the Schoolmen and the Renaissance. In belonging somewhere in the school of Duns Scotus, just as Luther belonged somewhere in the school of William of Ockham, Calvin's roots are shown to be in part in the long tradition of mediaeval theology.[2] But just as Luther's is a transformed Ockhamism, so is Calvin scarcely to be called a Scotist. Yet the fact remains. Apart from his selective reception of the thought of his teachers, he would not be the particular theologian John Calvin.

These remarks about the relation of Calvin to his past – to the tradition to which, however critically, he remained loyal – enable us to say something about the nature of the Reformation, and the debate about Bible and tradition that emerged

---

[1] Calvin is better described as an exponent of tradition than as a traditionalist, at least in the pejorative sense of that word.

[2] Torrance, *The Hermeneutics of John Calvin.*

from it. The dispute between Catholic and Protestant was, and remains, one about whether the Reformation was a return to the high road or the leading of parts of the church into a wilderness of error. The metaphor of the road provides us with a way of expressing one meaning of the word 'tradition'. It concerns the way the church bears herself in relation to the past. It thus concentrates attention on the actions of receiving, criticising, and passing on. That is one way of describing, defining almost, an aspect of tradition as the process in which human beings appropriate that which they receive from others – parents, teachers, ministers, etc. – in their past. Here attention is concentrated on certain human actions of reception, appropriation, and response; on a process.

We shall later explore something of the character of this process. But to clarify the general situation, we require the assistance of a second metaphor: that of the organism. Now that image has a history which underlies some theories of development and therefore of tradition. As time passes, it may suggest, like a plant growing larger or a child growing up, the content of doctrine becomes enriched. Here we reach a place where the ideas of revelation and of tradition begin to impinge directly upon one another. If revelation is something given in the beginning – as undoubtedly one dimension of it is, the faith once for all delivered to the saints – then it may be argued that through tradition what began as a seed or a seedling is enabled to expand without falsifying its beginnings. Tradition is thus a process of enrichment, and it might be argued that certain doctrines, for example – contentiously – the ontological priesthood of the ordained or the person of Mary as co-redeemer, are natural organic developments of the original revelation. That metaphor last century received, as is well known, a development by John Henry Newman in the context of the history of disputes between Catholic and Protestant.[3]

---

[3] John Henry Newman, *An Essay on the Development of Doctrine* (Harmondsworth: Penguin Books, 1974). This reference must not be taken to suggest that Newman was satisfied with all that was in this respect claimed by the church to which he converted.

It is worth observing, however, that the same image can be used to very different effect. The organism might become diseased, and require surgery; or it might simply grow too many branches, or branches in the wrong places, and require pruning. As will be recognised, that is a more biblical use of the metaphor, less contaminated by ideas of automatic evolution that always tempted the nineteenth century, and tempt ours still.[4] But, however it is used, the metaphor allows a significantly different aspect of tradition to come under consideration in the dispute between the divided churches. It concerns not so much the action of passing on, but what we do with the content while it is in our hands. Attention is concentrated more on that which is passed on – the content – and less on the process of transmission. According to this metaphor, the Reformation was either a necessary piece of pruning or wanton vandalism (or, to be sure, something of each). Whichever way one takes with that question, there can be little doubt that there is a process of adding and pruning, and that the church's view of the content of the faith that is received does vary as time passes.

All this shows that the matter is far more complicated than being simply one of Bible against tradition. Both sides in the dispute grant authority to both, albeit in different ways. Nor is it simply a matter of a dispute about whether the Bible and the tradition can be or are treated as complementary or rival *sources* of revelation. The differences are in large part about how revelation is appropriated, interpreted and transmitted. It is very much a question of the way in which different aspects are weighted in relation to one another.

What questions arise in all this? Chief among them are those of whether there is an unchangeable inner core or content to the Christian faith, what it contains and what is its character. What, if any, is the central *revelation*, the faith once for all delivered to the saints? Are there certain beliefs, propositions

---

[4] In *Systematic Theology* Volume 1 (reprinted, Grand Rapids: Eerdmans, 1989), p. 118, Charles Hodge refers to 'the modern theory of the organic development of the Church. This modern theory is avowedly founded on the pantheistic principles of Schelling and Hegel'.

or credal confessions, however the matter is put, which are in some sense revealed, and without any of which the Christian faith would no longer be recognisable as the Christian faith? That is the question that has been forced on the church by much modern thought, which for the first time since the Patristic era has called everything into question. One could say that the question of heresy in its original sense is being asked again, because in question is not the political matter of the peace of Christendom, which inevitably dominated even if it did not determine sixteenth-century debate, but the more centrally theological ones of what is and is not authentic Christianity and of how we decide what is. For the purposes of this discussion of tradition, I will take it as a working hypothesis that without certain beliefs, about God, Christ, salvation, the church and the work of the Spirit, Christianity would not be recognisably continuous with what it once was. It would not be a pruned plant, but a different one; there would not be tradition in any recognisable sense, but rupture. Judgement will differ about where the break comes. For some Catholic Anglicans, for example, it comes with the ordination of women, while for some extreme liberals even the existence of God is in question. But it is surely beyond question that there is such a possibility, wherever it be located.

II   *Towards a conception of tradition*

So far in the argument two images, the journey and the organism, have been used in an attempt to illustrate the nature of tradition. Before moving to matters of substance, let us try to understand the matter more conceptually. The problem of tradition is the problem of the authority of the past over the present. Here we reach a similar problem to that met in Lecture 2. There the problem was the authority of the other; here it is the authority of the past that is in question. That is why the value of tradition is rejected by the exponents of certain forms of modern ideology, as a denial of autonomy. But what is the underlying question? The question of tradition is the question of time, and of the way we live in it. One's concept of tradition therefore depends on one's concept of time, and this means that matters of major theological moment are at issue.

The enquiry can be opened up by means of an affirmation that involves a number of theological assumptions about the relation of eternity to time: that the future is what validates tradition. That is, it is to be hoped, not a general assertion, of the kind to be found in much modern theology, about the priority of the future, but a particular indication of the character of finite existence, not only of our theology and our ecclesial practice, but of all our science and art. The truth of all forms of culture, sacred and profane, whether we have built of brick or with straw, will finally come to be known at the end of all things, at their judgement (1 Cor. 3.10–15). Truth is in that respect the daughter of eternity. But she is also the daughter of time, for the passing of time, and the pruning of tradition, leave us with provisional answers to the questions of whether and in what sense the things we have received are true. It follows that the truly difficult question for those of us who live in the midst of time, between the resurrection of Christ and his return, is: what are we to make in the meantime of what we have received from the past, and, in our context, especially the biblical and churchly past, and how are we to judge both it and the developments we make of it?

An approach to an answer can be made through some observations on tradition in general, because in certain important respects theological and churchly tradition reveals the same kind of social shape as other forms of tradition. There are similarities to be found between the part that it plays in all kinds of different communities. First, a general definition of a kind. Tradition is a form of relation between people, in which those in the present receive from those in their past something that is either necessary or valuable – or intended so to be – for their life. That does not, of course, rule out all kinds of variations: the old can receive from the young, if the young have experience and skill lacking to the old. But the paradigm remains that according to which the older and wiser, or the previous generation, pass on skills, techniques, wisdom or knowledge to the young and inexperienced, such as the techniques of drawing or the skills of classical ballet.

One clear example of the way in which tradition operates as a way of relation between people is to be found in Michael Polanyi's account of the operation of scientific communities. Of crucial importance is his observation that it is no accident that major minds often produce pupils who also do important work, for they pass on to them the personal skills without which there is no knowledge at all. 'A society which wants to preserve a fund of personal knowledge must submit to tradition.'[5] For Polanyi, tradition is the crucial factor in the advance of knowledge that we call science, so that tradition in science is very different from traditionalism. Stanley Hauerwas has made a similar point about the way traditions work socially and politically. The modernist view that 'the only alternative to the conservative option is to find a rational basis for social organisation which is tradition free', Hauerwas sees to involve capture 'by a tradition that is more tyrannical because it has the pretense of absolute rationality'. In contrast, he argues that 'substantive traditions are not at odds with reason but are the bearers of rationality and innovation'.[6] Tradition, accordingly, in so far as it is salutary and not oppressive or simply mistaken, is, as a form of positive relatedness of present to past and future, the bearer of sedimented wisdom.

The heart of what we call tradition is to be found in relations between people which serve to form who and what they are. It is a process of giving and receiving in which the very shape of our being is at stake. It is in general unproblematic until for one reason or another it is called into question, when traditionalism and anti-traditionalism can become two sides of the same coin, two opposite ways of responding to a felt crisis, as at the Reformation and as in today's disputes about the nature of art. There is in all this no suggestion intended that this is a simple matter, or that there is a uniformity in the way things happen. The controversies resulting from the work of Thomas Kuhn demonstrate that tradition in science operates episodically, and often the tradition is advanced by means of a

[5] Polanyi, *Personal Knowledge*, p. 53.
[6] Stanley Hauerwas, *A Community of Character. Toward a Constructive Christian Social Ethic* (Notre Dame and London: University of Notre Dame Press, 1981), p. 26.

response to a crisis of tradition.[7] A positive assessment of the value of tradition cannot rule out lurches in which perhaps major innovations are made.[8]

When we speak of tradition we are, then, speaking of something universal to the human condition. Indeed, we could almost formulate a law of tradition: that for all the lurches and 'revolutions', the most secure and rational forms of progress and innovation are to be found where there is a fundamental trust in the tradition in which one stands, whether that be science, drama or theology: that it has to be carried on, however radical some changes have to be.[9] That was certainly the view of the Reformers, and its truth depends on the fact that without some positive relation to those in our past we are unable to build upon their wisdom, and so are without secure orientation to the future.

But – and here we come to basic differences between churchly and other traditions – one must also acknowledge

[7] A particularly interesting intervention in the debate about the nature of the 'scientific revolution' is that of Amos Funkenstein, *Theology and the Scientific Imagination from the Middle Ages to the Seventeenth Century* (Princeton: Princeton University Press, 1986).

[8] Whatever is made of the epistemological aspects of Kuhn's theory posited in *The Structure of Scientific Revolutions,* it is clear that there are times when there are major disruptions of the scientific tradition, when new, or new uses of, concepts come into use in such a way that he at least would speak of revolution. One could probably use that kind of language of the emergence of relativity theory early this century. Yet it must be observed that Einstein himself pays tribute not only to his predecessors in his revolution but also to Newton whose rule he is sometimes supposed to have overthrown. Einstein regards himself as belonging in the same scientific tradition as Newton. (See *The World as I See It.*) It is also often pointed out that the communist rulers of Russia were not so very different in their patterns of behaviour from their tsarist predecessors, while predictions of a strongly autocratic form of rule are already being made for their supposedly more democratic successors. And to complicate the matter still further, we should not forget Barth's observation that the highly traditionalist Anselm believed in the possibility of progress in theology. Similarly, the Reformation and Tractarianism were alike in various respects both highly innovative and highly traditionalist movements.

[9] The response of theology in the nineteenth century to the crisis of the Enlightenment is here highly instructive. A whole series of theologians of genius whose relation to their Christian and Enlightenment past was distinctively different saved a tradition that ought, 'rationally', to have disappeared.

differences in the way tradition works in different disciplines and cultures. The shape that a particular tradition takes corresponds to the content with which it is occupied. As the practices and interests of – say – scientists and historians differ, so will the way their traditions move. It is in this respect that Christian theology is different from them all. As some uses of the organic metaphor and the notion of pruning suggest, the Johannine notion of the vine in particular, we are in theology concerned not simply with a developing, albeit episodically developing, human tradition, but with a difference in category of that which is handed over from one generation to another, and, indeed, of the character of the ones who hand over and receive. The image of the vine is fundamentally christological in its form, and so is tied to Jesus Christ. Once the question of historical revelation comes into view, of the faith once for all delivered to the saints, there is, to use the cliché, a different ball game.

III　*Tradition and history*

To begin to play it, one necessity is a realisation that in the tradition of Christian theology, particularity has a different role to play from the one it plays in other fields of human culture. The relation between the universal and the particular is radically different from that in science. This can be seen if we ask the question, *What* is transmitted through tradition? One answer is that in science there is a body of ever-developing doctrine, sometimes with major changes of direction, focus, etc.; skills; a *morality*. In the arts? There are skills, a history (there it is like science). In the Christian church? In the first place, we should not exaggerate the differences between the church as community and the various other communities – of art and science – with which we are concerned. This also is the realm of the handing on of skills, approaches to our predecessors and a morality. (In fact, some would make that the heart of what it is to be in the church.)[10] But, as has already

---

[10] Whatever may have happened to the universities since they ceased to be theological schools for clerks and became the focuses for secular teaching and research, it becomes increasingly clear that many of the things theologians do continue to be similar to the things that others do. And whatever we make of that

been suggested, it is the differences which make our problem what it distinctively is.[11] We do not merely hand on traditions in a historical albeit episodic way, as happens in science. There is also a sense in which we hand over a relation to a unique and unrepeatable history: to historical revelation, biblically formulated. That Einstein wrote his famous papers while working in an office in Switzerland may add to the romance of the history of scientific discovery, but it adds nothing to the traditions of scientific knowledge. That Jesus died on the cross at a particular time and place is definitive for the shape that tradition takes in the church. The question of tradition is in large measure the problem of how the traditions about Jesus are handed on and who has the right to judge which are the true interpretations.

To seek enlightenment we must return to the historical beginnings. The difficulties about that arise from two related

---

case, there are many respects in which churchly traditioning bears the same kind of marks as the traditioning in other forms of culture.

[11] There is a case for saying that in our situation there are two focuses of discussion about the character of tradition, and in only one of them is the sociological shape of traditioning radically different from that of other communities of practice. The difference is that while science, for example, is a culturally successful – or rather, perhaps better, confident – form of practice, in the West the church is not. At the Reformation, the Western church's confidence in the reliability of the way her traditions were transmitted became undermined. This was either because Luther and others were sinful schismatics seeking to elevate their private judgement over the wisdom of the community, or because the community had become so corrupt that its practice came rightly into question. Whatever the rights and wrongs of Luther's behaviour, the facts that indulgences were sold and that heretics were burned at the stake are evidence that there were at least major irregularities in the transmission of the gospel of the crucified one. It is possible that some signs of a death of a living tradition were already evident in some forms of scholasticism. Werner Elert remarked that after the late patristic period christological debate tended to become reduced to the reproduction and elaboration of formulae. The ecclesiastical tradition became such that certain elements of a live theological tradition became lost. Werner Elert, *Der Ausgang der altkirchlichen Christologie* (Berlin: Lutherisches Verlagshaus, 1957), pp. 10f., 22, 64, 235. There was very little innovative christology that was also true to Chalcedon in the mainstream of Western theology until relatively recent times, the crucial influence being the rise of Socinianism. Much modern christology, indeed, has

problems. The first is that the meaning of the unique and unrepeatable history is not transparent. The second is that, because it shapes or is in some way held to be constitutive for the shape that Christian communities take in time, its interpretation raises the question of authority. Who best can interpret the historic tradition in the modern world? Universal or local church? Hans Küng or the pope? These show the shape of modern difficulties, for they derive from very different theologies of revelation and tradition, as Robert Jenson has recently shown.[12] In the remainder of the lecture, however, I shall concentrate on the first of the problems, the meaning of the unique and unrepeatable history in relation to tradition, simply from time to time allowing matters of authoritative interpretation to come into view.

The most easily recognisable account of the working of tradition in the New Testament is perhaps to be found in Paul's two narratives in his first Letter to Corinth. Here both of our questions, of interpretation and of authority, come into view. In his treatment of them, there is explicit reference to the fact that Paul passes on what he has received. Tradition is, as we have seen, a form of personal relation taking shape in time, in this case between Paul's teachers and himself, and then between him and the church. The first narrative (1 Cor. 11) is a tradition of the words and actions *of* Jesus at the Last Supper,

---

lived from the denial of the classical tradition. For better or worse, and mainly for worse, the Reformation's call of the church back to the high road in an unfortunate way spawned the Enlightenment's and modernity's critique of the validity of traditional revelation. In this area, then, the differences between theology and other cultural traditions derive mainly from the calling of that tradition into question, and not from their radically different sociological shape. Interesting here is the fact that in recent times there has developed a similar battering of confidence in other non-scientific forms of tradition. With the loss of belief in certain of the Christian doctrines that have been integral to Western culture has come a loss of some of the presuppositions that have shaped Western art, so that some of the debates about painting and music resemble those between theological modernists and traditionalists. And even science is beginning to feel the chill winds of modernist, anti-traditionalist scepticism.

[12] Robert W. Jenson, *Unbaptized God. The Basic Flaw in Ecumenical Theology* (Minneapolis: Fortress Press, 1992).

the second (1 Cor. 15) of the gospel that he has received *about* the one who spoke and acted at the Supper, that he was put to death for our sins and raised to life on the third day according to the scriptures (v. 3). In their relation is gathered a whole nest of problems concerning tradition in Christianity, but above all it raises the question of the relation of content and expression; of history – of what happened – and of interpretation – of the words in which the history is articulated and transmitted. So far as the latter is concerned, it appears likely that, as Dodd has argued, there is something like a shared content in the main lines of the early Christian preaching:

> [T]wo facts have come into view: first is that within the New Testament there is an immense range of variety in the interpretation that is given to the *kerygma*; and, secondly, that in all such interpretation the essential elements are kept in view. Indeed, the farther we move from the primitive modes of expression, the more decisively is the central purport of it affirmed. With all the diversity of the New Testament writings, they form a unity in their proclamation of the one Gospel.[13]

Tradition accordingly took form as the passing on of a broadly unified group of confessions about God, Christ and salvation. We might say, and here we do reach the question of revelation, that what was passed on looks suspiciously like a common deposit of faith expressed in varied propositional form: the faith once for all delivered – traditioned – to the saints. As Paul's writing both here and elsewhere shows, however, the tradition did not come authoritatively interpreted. What was meant by resurrection was clearly a matter of dispute at Corinth, one indeed that had major implications for the living of the Christian life.[14] What is made of the tradition is a matter of continuing dispute, and is relevant to a theology of revelation because the biblical writings here are themselves shown to be

---

[13] C. H. Dodd, *The Apostolic Preaching and its Developments* (London: Hodder & Stoughton, third edition, 1963), p. 74. For Dodd's treatment of the other theme of the verse, the scriptures, see *According to the Scriptures. The Substructure of New Testament Theology* (London: Collins, 1965. First edition 1952).

[14] In fact, and interestingly, we have here a trailer for the very question that Irenaeus would thrash out with the Gnostics in years to come.

part of a tradition of interpretation of that which is in certain respects prior to them.

Paul's dispute with the church over the celebration of the Lord's Supper, on the other hand, concerns the way in which the tradition was received and embodied in the life of the Christian community. Alongside the question of revelation is therefore that of ethics: of the authority of the narratives and confessions which are handed on from one generation to another for the ordering of the church's life.[15] In both realms, interpretation and ethics, the tradition is authoritative because it is tied up with divine revelation: the self-manifestation of God to the church in Jesus Christ. Not even the most conservative Protestant would, I think, question that point, that the tradition, meaning that which is handed over from the apostles, is authoritative for the faith and life of the church.[16] Where, then, is the problem? It concerns the way in which the generally agreed revelation is interpreted and handed on by those who follow the prophets and apostles: the way in which revelation is mediated by tradition.

Two recent writings have attempted to relativise the post-Reformation problem of the relative weight of scripture and tradition in the mediation of revelation. The first comes from the documents of the Second Vatican Council. 'The Tradition that comes from the apostles makes progress in the Church, with the help of the Holy Spirit.'[17] Now although this may appear to involve almost a reifying, if not personification, of tradition, and more than a hint of a naively organic view of development, one particular supporting argument is important in suggesting that revelation is to be understood as prior to both scripture and tradition, so that

---

[15] 1 Corinthians 8 is another example of how the handed-on traditions of the faith – one God, the Father, and one Lord, Jesus Christ – must be interpreted if they are rightly to shape the life of the community.

[16] Those who might want to deny it in quite so simplistic a form would be those who have imbibed a suspicion of authoritative tradition from the traditions of modernity.

[17] 'Dogmatic Constitution on Divine Revelation', *Vatican Council II. The Conciliar and Post-Conciliar Documents*, edited by A. Flannery OP (Leominster: Fowler Wright, 1975), p. 754.

both are to be understood as responses to the same divine reality. 'Sacred Scripture is the speech of God as it is put down in writing under the breath of the Holy Spirit. And tradition transmits in its entirety the Word of God which has been entrusted to the apostles . . .'.[18] Here a way out of inherited disputes is offered by a concept of the word of God or divine revelation as prior to both its scriptural expression and its transmission by means of tradition.

But the weakness in the formulation indicates where questions still have to be asked. Does the tradition – *can* the tradition – transmit the word of God 'in its entirety'? There seems to be reason to believe that the content is more elusive than that, and that is why some doubt should be expressed about the Council's confidence in the Magisterium's capacity to speak the final word on the interpretation of revelation.[19] Although the underlying concern of the Council is right, so that it is important to maintain tradition in good repair, there are limits to any human authority's capacity to anticipate the

[18] Ibid., p. 755.

[19] The chief reason is that history appears to demonstrate that such arrogation of authority to élites, and that would include the liberal élites that sometimes command the high places of Protestant churches, fails to allow truth to be the daughter of time and rather represents attempts to anticipate too confidently the judgement of God. It is also the case that authoritarianism derives in part from a lack of trust that the faithful can and should be the judges of the authorities. This is not to idealise some form of democracy, but rather to suggest that the judgement of God be allowed to take its course and not be anticipated by legal action. I have used elsewhere John Owen's appeal to 1 Cor. 11.19, that heresies are for 'the manifesting of those that are approved, not the destroying of those that are not', as well as 2 Timothy's instruction that we should 'wait with all patience on those that oppose themselves, if at any time God will give them repentance . . .'. 'The Church on Earth: The Roots of Community', *On Being the Church. Essays on the Christian Community*, edited by C. E. Gunton and D. W. Hardy (Edinburgh: T&T Clark, 1989), pp. 48–80 (p. 54). It may be painful, and involve the toleration of what may appear to be schismatic movements. (Toleration, by definition, implies disapproval.) Equally, it may involve schism. Opponents of the ordination of women are right to consider leaving the Church of England if they believe that the change means in effect that the church no longer lives and proclaims the gospel of Christ. I think that they are wrong on that particular issue, though not on all their arguments, because the traditions of feminism or liberal human rights theory are not authoritative for the church.

judgement of eternity. History does suggest that those communities who put themselves outside the historically transmitted gospel disappear, even though only in the long run. As Keynes said, in the long run we are all dead, but interpreted theologically that is to say that God can be left to have the last word in his own time.[20] If truth is indeed the daughter of time, there are ways in which we must not seek to hurry tradition, whether progressively or otherwise.

The mistake made by the church of Christendom was in effect to replace the authority of the *content* of tradition – of that which is handed on – by forms of ecclesiastical authority. To put it otherwise we can say that the distortion comes not from any form of churchly authority, but from premature confidence in it. In this context, it is possible, though less likely these days, to idealise the early church, and I do not wish to do so.[21] Yet there is in the early period plentiful evidence that the

---

The reason why we should not attempt to rashly to execute the judgement of God is indeed a matter of eschatology. Nearly all the most discreditable actions of churchly institutions, and I include the history of Catholic and Protestant churches alike, flow from an improper anticipation of eschatology. But, more than that, it is also a matter of history, of the way God works in time. The fact that God operates historically by means of the human life and cross of Jesus carries with it the implication that he shapes history but only in a way that can be called patient. Time is allowed to take its course, or rather time is shaped non-coercively, once again in clear contradiction of the coercion often applied by the self-proclaimed agents of the tradition. We may not attempt to hurry the divine action. Behind this christological argument is a strange and surely significant verbal repetition, that the language of tradition is also the language of God's giving up his only Son for the sins of the world.

[20] Two historical examples can be cited in support of that general thesis. The first is the view of even sceptical historians that if Arianism had won the day, the church would have disappeared into the religious melting pot of the Roman world. (The same would go for the Arianising theologies of religious pluralism of those such as John Hick.) The second is the even more hackneyed illustration of the fact that English Presbyterianism became unitarian in the eighteenth and nineteenth centuries and to all intents and purposes disappeared. (The Presbyterians who joined the United Reformed Church in 1972 were for the most part of Scottish provenance.)

[21] When we defend the importance of tradition, we should not forget some of the things that have been done in its name, including the crucifixion of Jesus. The behaviour of early defenders of tradition, and Alexandria appears to win the

authoritative tradition was best defended by argument rather than violence or legal process. The greatness of Irenaeus is that despite plentiful appeal to the received tradition, the strength of his case, and one reason that we still read him, is for his interpretation of the tradition by argument, if highly polemical argument. And there is a further reason for interest in him here, for we owe to him a conception of the centrality of the rule of faith (or, interestingly, that which he sometimes refers to as the rule of truth),[22] and its primacy over both scripture and tradition.

Just as in the first lecture it was argued that we should not dismiss out of hand the propositional aspects of revelation, so here it will be contended that we should take seriously the notion of what came to be called the deposit of faith, something given that is to be handed on from one generation of the church to another if Christianity is to remain truly itself. But all the difference in the world is made by the different ways in which it is conceived, and that brings us to the second recent resource for our discussion, an article by Professor T. F. Torrance. For him, as for the Second Vatican Council, the heart of the matter is divine self-revelation, 'the incarnate self-communication of God in Jesus Christ mediated after the Ascension and Pentecost through the Apostles'.[23] The heart of the matter is not, we might gloss, particular formulations but a personal relationship taking form at a particular time in human history. Speaking of improved understandings of these things on both sides of divided Western Christendom, Torrance writes:

----

prize for the combination of great theologians and ruthless politicians, was at times appalling. Prestige's defence of the indefensible appears not to be offered in a spirit of irony. Describing Cyril's use of violent methods to persecute heretics and Jews, he makes two quite priceless comments: 'Archbishop Cyril did not occupy himself with civil administration to any greater extent than did Archbishop Laud'; and 'Such are the incidental perils to be balanced against the incalculable advantages of effective Church establishment.' *Fathers and Heretics, Being the Bampton Lectures for 1940* (London: SPCK, 1940), pp. 151, 153.

[22] For example, Irenaeus, *Adv. Haer.* III.11.1.

[23] T. F. Torrance, 'The Deposit of Faith', *Scottish Journal of Theology* 36 (1983), 1–28 (2).

Thus in Evangelical and Catholic churches alike the major emphasis on the Deposit of Faith came now to be thrown upon the objective and living Reality of Christ himself and his saving acts as they took the field in the form of the Word of Truth of the gospel which continuously begets the Church in history as the Body of Christ in the world.[24]

It is here that we can achieve a measure of understanding of the different ways of construing the relation between the revelation that is Jesus Christ the Truth, on the one hand, and the propositions in which the Christian faith is expressed, the truth of the faith, on the other. We saw in the previous lecture that the problem of revelation and inspiration is less intractable if we treat the divine action in Jesus and the words in which scripture articulates it as being in an intrinsic rather than extrinsic relation to one another. The same is the case here of the relation between the revelation that is the basis for tradition and the words in which it is variously transmitted through time. Torrance shows that there is in this respect all the difference in the world between Irenaeus' and Tertullian's ways of formulating the relation. Tertullian tends to an extrinsic view which is significantly different from Irenaeus' conception. 'While for Irenaeus the canon of truth was in fact the *Truth* itself . . . for Tertullian the rule of faith was consistently regarded as a fixed formula of truth for belief, which he claimed had been instituted by Christ himself and had been handed down entire and unchanged from the apostles . . .'.

The point is that the intrinsic relation between revelation and its expression is obstructed, not preserved, by supposing that there is 'an "irreformable" set of revealed doctrines which constituted the "sum and substance" of all that is learned of God . . .'.[25] As Torrance points out, the development represented by Tertullian has led to an increasing tension between scripture and tradition, not their appropriate correlation. 'The effect of this was to make the rule of faith no more and no less than a deposit of doctrinal propositions,

[24] Ibid., 25.
[25] Ibid., 15.

and indeed to make the very concept of the rule of faith itself into a doctrine.'[26] Forsyth put it similarly:

> If Christian truth were a plexus of doctrine, our certainty would rest on one kind of authority (which would probably be a finally authoritative Church). But Christian truth is not that; it is not propositional or statutory; it is not a gift, a revelation, of formal law, but of spiritual reality, divine life, personal grace.[27]

To claim an intrinsic relation between revelatory history and credal affirmation or theological articulation is not to deny that there is also a space between the two which invalidates any claim for completeness or ultimacy for any particular form of words.

The consequence of Tertullian's misunderstanding is that because a personal relation is *replaced* by propositions rather than being that which is expressed more or less adequately by them, the tradition of authoritative interpretation becomes by turns both 'static' and innovative in a way not licensed by the truth. It is on the one hand too conservative and resistant to innovation; and, on the other, it claims too much for its magisterial development of that which it has received. There thus develops a strange mixture of a tradition that is extrinsic to the canon of truth as Torrance conceives it, and yet claims a relation that is *too* immediate, too intrinsic. This returns us to what has concerned us in and since the first lecture. It is no wonder that propositional forms have come into question if they are identified in some way with revelation. That is, indeed, an invitation to be 'static', and indeed to think of the faith as a finite series of propositions to which new ones may be added according to the demands of revelation in different historical contexts. But if propositions are secondary and therefore dependent for their truth on the personal presence of God to the world which is revelation; and, further, if their form at any given time is also dependent upon the gift of the Spirit who

---

[26] Ibid., 15–16. Perhaps this is what lies behind the Second Vatican Council's problematic statement that tradition transmits the word of God 'in its entirety'. It is also a reason why the concept of 'revealed truths' should be resisted. That is not what is intended by the defence of propositions in the first lecture.

[27] Forsyth, *The Principle of Authority*, p. 53.

mediates the revelation in words appropriate to different historical contexts, we need not be afraid of them. What is necessary is that the propositions should be understood to be *both* secondary *and* in intrinsic relation to that which they articulate.

In the previous lecture an argument was developed that there is an intrinsic connection between the revelatory action of God in Christ and the words in which, by the Spirit, the New Testament writers came to express it. In this lecture, the complementary suggestion is being made that the relation between revelation and the words in which the church has come to express its truth is not only intrinsic, but also in an important respect open. We are indeed concerned to express truths, but truths which are themselves expressive of that which reaches us in and as a person, Jesus Christ, the one Word of God. The relation of intrinsicality and openness is therefore different in the two cases of scripture and tradition. The distinctive placing of the contemporary of revelation, the apostle, is the advantage of a sharing in the story, of, so to speak, being part of the divine action. The secondary character of later tradition derives from the fact that it operates in continuing dependence upon the words of the prophets and apostles. Whatever it may mean to say that the church or her representatives are apostolic, it cannot mean that she is in the same relation to revelation as the apostles. But that need not exclude an intrinsic relationship, too, because without our predecessors in the tradition we should be unable to appropriate that which the prophets and apostles mediate. By living in the words they hand on to us, we become able, through them, to receive that which they mediate.

The relationship of the prophets and apostles to revelation is a relative authority, and, with Torrance, we must affirm that there is no 'one-to-one correspondence', to use the fashionable jargon, between formulation and reality. 'In this event a distinction between the substance of the Faith and the substance of doctrine was called for, in adoring respect for the Truth of God revealed in Jesus Christ.'[28] But that does not

[28] Torrance, 'Deposit of Faith', 26.

entail that we can cope without the tradition descending from them, for the church's tradition is, in its turn, relative to what we receive from them, through the process of giving and receiving which is of the essence of the church. The *mediation* of the prophets and apostles is necessarily itself *mediated* through a process of human giving and reception. Are there, then, degrees of mediation? That will be the question asked in our next and final lecture.

IV   *Conclusion*

The problem of tradition is the problem of the mediation of the past. Because of modern difficulties with the concept, immediacy becomes in much modern theology an alternative to tradition. The Bible becomes the trigger of some immediate experience rather than the mediator of teaching, and this is where serious questions have to be asked of Bultmann, and perhaps of Barth. That is to say, revelation for Bultmann tends to be of a God not tied to the historical past that is Jesus of Nazareth, while for Barth the impression is at times given that his humanity is somewhat secondary in revelatory weight. In that respect we can be more sympathetic than was the early twentieth century with the quest of the historical Jesus, which thus may be understood as an attempt to be true to the method of tradition. It was, to be sure, vitiated by its second salient feature, an attempt to achieve that mediation apart from the mediation of the church's tradition of teaching, for the quest was in large part an attempt to go back beyond ecclesiastical tradition to some hidden core ignored by it but discoverable by the methods of free rational enquiry. The Jesus of the quest is not the Jesus mediated by scripture, as Hans Frei has shown beyond dispute.[29] The quest's main mistake is that of all rationalism, to ignore the place of God the Spirit in all our intellectual enterprises. The Spirit in this context is the one who works through and in time, and that means that although we may and must be critical of tradition, as the action of fallible

---

[29] In that respect, there is much in common between the liberal 'quest' and some liberation theology, understood as another attempt to have a historical Jesus apart from his taught significance mediated through the tradition.

and sinful human beings, we may not lay aside the means which God has himself chosen.

Here orthodox Catholicism and orthodox Reformation theology have concerns in common: the preservation of the 'deposit of faith'. The Reformation protest is not against tradition as a form of personal relation – as we have seen, the Reformers were traditionalist in certain central respects – but against the fabrication of traditions not consistent with biblical teaching and against premature claims to judge what is the truth.[30] Why then is tradition so important? Because even though Jesus is, as risen and ascended, not in the past – that is, even though the church's faith is in a present Lord, known in worship – that Lord cannot be identified apart from the Jesus of scriptural description mediated through the tradition of interpretation which is theology. Tradition is necessary because the present Jesus is the one who at a particular time in our past lived a certain life, died upon the cross and was raised from the dead for our justification, and as the Lord both absent and present is mediated in different ways by scripture and its tradition of interpreters.

Tradition in the church, then, is a process of gift and reception in which the deposit of faith – the teaching and ethics of the Christian community – is received, interpreted and handed on through time. As such, when it is true giving and reception, it realises[31] the Father's giving of his Son, the Son's self-giving to death and indeed the very life of God of which they are the economic expression. It is for reasons such as this that we should maintain a strong view of the centrality of the particulars which have been handed down to us, to and through the biblical writers, but a less enthusiastic endorsement of the way in which the authority of the exponents of that tradition has intruded upon its due and non-coercive transmission. Churchly authority has not always been the authority of grace, and all too often has taken the form of the expression of coercive power. The conclusion to draw is that the greater

---

[30] That is why Barth is right to see in Roman Catholicism and Liberal Protestantism two aspects of the same human attempt to control revelation.

[31] The word used in the first draft of this lecture, 'reflects', is not nearly strong enough.

weight one can throw upon the faith once for all delivered to the saints, by which is meant the confession of Jesus and his meaning as the revelation of God, found alike in the apostolic preaching and the rule of faith, the less we have to trust in the judgement of offices, whether Holy or Protestant administrative. It is a recipe, one might say, either for chaos or for allowing the wheat and tares to grow together until the harvest. Thus truth is indeed the daughter of time: the time God gives his church for the faithful reception and transmission of the gospel.

Lecture 6

Varieties of mediation: Towards a theology of revelation

I   *The story so far*

The previous five lectures, seen in retrospect, have taken the form of a series of explorations of different ways in which revelation can be understood to be mediated. The later lectures developed a greater concentration on what can be said to be the centre of it all, the personal act of divine self-revelation which is Jesus Christ. We began with the capacity of propositions to mediate revelation, then moved to the world and its capacities for revelation of both the creature and the creator, before, through the Bible and tradition, moving into the centre. Tradition came last, not because it is prior to the Bible – quite the reverse – but because it enabled us to gain a clearer view of the centre: that from which both it and the Bible take their meaning as mediators of revelation. In the lectures the question of mediation arose in the following ways:

1. In the first lecture the question was raised by means of a discussion of the function of propositions in theology. Propositions may not be revelation, but they may in a derivative sense be revelatory. We address God as 'thou', through Christ and in the Spirit. But although in our primary relationship to one another we address each other by name, or as 'you', it is quite proper sometimes to speak of one another in the third person – for example in commending a friend to a third

person. (Not so commendably, by gossip.) Similarly, although we may believe God to have spoken to us or to others revealingly and in person, we communicate the faith propositionally in such a way that others too may find in what we say – 'Jesus died for our sins', for example – something revelatory of the fact that he indeed did, and lives to make intercession for us. At least, that is the way in which it has often happened in practice. In this sense, revelation is a form of personal relation of God to the world conveyed by forms of words, and it is that according to which the author of Ephesians speaks of the revelation of a mystery. 'Mystery' in that case means the communication of a teaching: 'that the Gentiles are fellow heirs, members of the same body, and partakers of the promise of Jesus Christ through the gospel' (3.6).

2. In the second lecture, the claim was made that all kinds of things are revelatory. They are in the first place not necessarily revelatory of God – we must not try to reach that place too soon – but of themselves, or of the order of things in the world. If we are to know anything, or anyone, they must in some respect be revealed to us. In that sense, Paul Tillich is right to say that anything can serve as a medium of revelation, even though it does not follow, as he sometimes may appear to suggest, that anything may serve as the vehicle of the revelation of God.[1] There is a general concept of revelation, and this implies, especially in the case of the revelation of non-personal things, that it is not wrong to hold that even this phenomenon is indicative of the agency of God, because it at least suggests a form of personal agency and relation. In this case, too, revelation, in being dependent on the personal action of God, is a form of personal relation, and indeed one in which we are enabled to know truths about the world. If even the general conception of revelation is indeed a *theological* doctrine, we should have to say that in this context it is an implication of God's creating and conserving activity: of his having made and of his continuing to hold the world in being in such a way that

[1] 'There is no reality, thing, or event which cannot become a bearer of the mystery of being and enter into a revelatory correlation.' Paul Tillich, *Systematic Theology* (London: Nisbet, 1968), Volume 1, p. 131.

meaningful interpretation of it may take place. A general conception of revelation articulates the fact that we can speak of the world because there is a sense in which we are first spoken to through it.

3. In the third lecture was raised the question of the revelation of God through the medium of created things. That is what has sometimes been known as general revelation. 'Forever singing as they shine / "The hand that made us is divine"': despite the rather rationalistic terms in which that hymn is written,[2] it witnesses a real truth, that by virtue of its internal structuring, rather than by its so-called 'sacramental' character, we may say that the world reveals its maker, just as it was Mozart's music as music, and not as making some ulterior point, that for Barth made it uniquely revelatory. What is the source of this belief? What grounds do we have for believing that God is revealed by the creation and that therefore the created order in some way serves as the medium of the revelation of God? If we are cautious of the traditional tendency to treat human reason as in some way a unique medium of revelation, and if the nature of creation as creation disqualifies that reason from seeking continuities between the worldly and the divine, the grounds may only be found in acts of self-revelation by the triune God, what is sometimes known as special revelation. Apart from the Bible and salvation in the Christ of whom it speaks – Christ the creator – we should be unable truly to recognise the revelation that is there. Unless we are given by God the Spirit through the medium of the Bible eyes to see, we cannot see what is before us. Thus although the Bible can be treated as a dead book, and too often is, it is better understood as the mediator of a form of personal relation, in that we read there the words of those authors who are in a unique personal relation to us because they are prophets and apostles.

4. It is as such – and now we move to the fourth lecture – that scripture, too, can be understood to be a medium of revelation. If we must rely on scripture's spectacles even for

[2] 'In reason's ear they all rejoice . . .'. From Joseph Addison, 'The spacious firmament on high'.

the knowledge that the world is *creation,* the question is raised of the sense in which scripture can be understood to be the medium also of special revelation: not just a general concept of revelation or general revelation, but a particular revelation without which we should not know the things that pertain to our salvation. Scripture is revelatory in that sense by virtue of the fact that it participates in those things – persons and events – that we call revelation. It emerges out of Israel's calling by and struggle with her God and out of that which happened by, with and to Jesus of Nazareth. Scripture is uniquely the medium of special revelation because Israel and Jesus are the historic agents by whose sending God engages in person with the evil that disfigures the world and blinds human eyes to what is there to be seen. Revelation in this sense is the opening of the eyes of the blind so that they may see the salvation achieved in Christ, but, despite the visual metaphor, it is an opening of the eyes by means of the ears.[3] It is in that way also that the New Testament itself uses the word, as for example in Galatians 1.12, where Paul says: 'I did not receive [my gospel] from man, nor was I taught it, but it came through a revelation (ἀποκαλύψεως) of Jesus Christ.'

5. Jesus for Paul was clearly a living and personal present reality who made himself known to him on the road to Damascus. But in other respects, and here we must be aware of the many senses of the word 'revelation', Paul received the gospel by the mediation of human agency rather than directly or immediately. And that is the situation of most, if not all, of the rest of us. Wherever Jesus is *now* – that is, quite independently of what we happen to believe about the ascended Christ present in the church and the world – we do not have a direct, unmediated relation to him, at least in the sense that the words which communicate his reality are firmly

---

[3] In this case too, we must hear in order to be able to see. See above Lecture 2, note 4. See Torrance, *The Hermeneutics of John Calvin*, pp. 38–9, cf. p. 89, for an interesting discussion of the influence on Calvin of John Major of Haddington. Major speaks of 'faith arising out of hearing' and of 'seeing in the Word'. Calvin 'made peculiarly his own the emphasis of Reuchlin that knowledge of God arises and is passed on *ex auditu* or *ab auditu*'.

anchored in the past. This means that because the texts are couched in the concepts of a particular era, they are relative to a particular historical context. God comes to language in the particularities of a culture. This means that the interpretation of the revelatory particulars is entrusted to particular people, who by handing on what they have received become what we call a tradition. As we saw, tradition is, before it is anything else, a form of personal relation, and we need the mediation of a tradition of interpretation if we are to receive revelation for what it is.

In all of these matters, we are in different ways concerned with personal relationships. Revelation is mediated by tradition as well as by propositions, the Bible and the rest, and we must not make the mistake of thinking that even propositions are necessarily impersonal. (Does not 'I love you' contain a propositional content?) The conclusion to be drawn from the variety and multiplicity of the forms of revelation is that different weight is to be attributed to different forms of mediation. Because revelation is centred on Jesus Christ, it is mediated by a variety of mediations which close on the Bible and that which it uniquely has to communicate. But because the point of all this discussion is to understand how the gospel may be mediated to us, today, in all its saving and renewing power, we must now turn to the question of what is the revelation that is at the centre of the mediations. That is what concerns us now.

Let us begin with a lesson from Lecture 4. Revelation proper is that which happened with and to those we call the priests, prophets and kings; and more especially, with and to the apostles. That is their peculiar form of personal relatedness, which is unrepeatable because of the unique divine action of God in which they were caught up. But the question this raises is: how can that unique personal relation be communicated to us, or *become* ours? In what kind of community are we with the prophets and apostles? (What is the relation here between communion and communication?) And can we speak of the revelation in which they participated as being communicable to those who are not prophets and apostles?

II   *Revelation and the economy of divine action*

As has already been suggested from time to time, it is important for us to bear always in mind that revelation is a secondary doctrine, in that its function is to preserve and explain the character of that which is revealed. There are various ways of understanding this. If we say, for example, that our primary relation to God is one of faith or trust, not of propositional knowledge or information, we are speaking not so much of revelation as of a form of present personal relationship, of a saving relationship. Therefore it follows that the doctrine of revelation is secondary in so far as it describes the conditions of our knowledge of God by identifying the origin in God himself of our knowledge of the God in whom we have faith. A similar point would be to say that revelation is largely to do with the epistemic, not the soteriological or experiential dimension of the Christian faith. Again, it could be said that the primary content of the Christian gospel is not a doctrine of revelation, but doctrines of creation, salvation and life in the church. All these suggest in different ways the limits which our concept must keep if the faith is not to be reduced to knowledge, or the conditions for theology confused with that of which we must speak.[4]

The content of Christianity is, as we have seen, expressed in the different formulations of the rule of faith, that is to say in the creeds and confessions which have variously and at different times been the church's response to historical needs and crises. And the content concerns not so much revelation as God, so that the time has come to engage with Ronald Thiemann's point that revelation should be in some way a function of the doctrine of God:

> *A doctrine of revelation is an account of God's identifiability.* That definition locates the doctrine within reflection on God's identity, i.e. within the doctrine of God, rather than in

---

[4] That is why there is always some truth in accusations that Barth *reduces* Christianity to revelation. He does not, but gives too many hostages to fortune in making it so prominent that it always threatens to usurp the place of the mistress of the house.

prolegomenal or methodological reflection. The Christian claim to revelation asserts that God is identifiable 1) within the narrative of Yahweh who raised Jesus from the dead, 2) through the narrative as the God of promise who in addressing his promise to the reader is recognised as *pro nobis* and *extra nos*, and 3) beyond the narrative as the one who, faithful to his promises, will fulfil his pledge to those whom he loves.[5]

There is much to be said for that account, but it requires limitation and specification in the light of the argument of these lectures. In the first place, we cannot, simply because we are afraid of foundationalism, avoid the epistemic dimensions of the doctrine. A non-foundationalist account of revelation would not rule out its largely, perhaps primarily, epistemic and even foundational function, as providing an account of the reasons one has to believe something. Foundationalism has been avoided in this account particularly by the argument of Lecture 2 that revelation is a universal cultural phenomenon that requires a trinitarian construction if it is to be satisfactorily understood. In the second place, while it is undoubtedly true that God identifies himself through the action of the Spirit to be the Father of our Lord Jesus Christ, the focus of that action, as is shown by those confessions on which the New Testament centres and which its writers receive and transmit to others, is the salvation brought by Jesus of Nazareth. *The centre is not divine self-identification but divine saving action.* Thus it is preferable to say that revelation is first of all a function of that divine action by which the redemption of the creation is achieved in such a way that human blindness and ignorance are also removed. To that extent the doctrine of revelation should be understood to be a function of the doctrine of salvation.

To say that, however, is not to limit revelation so much as to delimit it, to centre it on the saving action of God in Christ who is the mediator also of creation. This bring us to the third point which can be made in relation to Thiemann's account, and it relates to his use of the category of narrative. Without

---

[5] Thiemann, *Revelation and Theology*, p. 153. Italics are in the original.

doubt, a doctrine of revelation centring on salvation does also centre on a narratively identified God. But if salvation is redemption of the creation, the centre cannot be divorced from that which circles about it. Accordingly, the focusing of revelation on the economy of salvation, if that is understood in a trinitarian matrix, involves necessary reference to the economy of creation, salvation and the final redemption of all things. Broadening the conspectus, it must therefore be said that revelation is a function of the divine economy as a whole. This means that the claim that revelation is primarily a function of the economy involves something wider than a narratively identified God, for non-narrative texts, like the Wisdom literature, are also to be regarded as means of making known God the creator. Much narrative theology is too tied to the old 'history of salvation' theology which tends to exclude due reference to creation. Revelation is therefore of a God who creates, conserves, saves, calls into the community of praise, and redeems; although, given that things are as they are, he is primarily and centrally revealed through his saving action.

It is in such a light that we must understand those biblical characterisations of revelation concerned with the disclosure of divine intent. As we have already seen, Ephesians offers a definitive example, but there is much to be learned also from characterisations of God's realisation of the kingdom in the Synoptic Gospels. The words and actions of Jesus there recorded make known the re-establishment of the rule of God that is realised through them, but also make clear the eschatological character of revelation. God's will to perfect the creation is in Jesus both re-inaugurated and declared. This has to be understood in twofold respect. In the first place, it is future eschatological: 'as you wait for the revealing of our Lord Jesus Christ' (1 Cor. 1.7); 'that the genuineness of your faith . . . may redound to praise and glory and honour at the revelation of Jesus Christ' (1 Pet. 1.7). The completion of revelation is yet to come. But, in the second place, the eschatology of the future is one that impinges on the present, no more so than in the divine saving action in Jesus of Nazareth. Because the completion of the eschatological intent is inaugurated in him, what happens there is also rightly described as revelation.

Thus, despite what is sometimes suggested, although it is in that respect an eschatological category, revelation, as a category of systematic theology, is also, and in a major way, to be understood in terms of that which we are granted to know in the midst of things. What happened in Israel and Jesus, anticipations of the end as they no doubt are, must yet be construed as truly giving a form of knowledge in the here and now: the knowledge of faith. As, then, we treat it in theology, it is very much the realised aspects of revelation with which we are concerned, because of the character of that with which we are concerned. That is why the meaning of the word 'revelation' has in these lectures been centred on the achievement of salvation in the life, death, resurrection and ascension of Jesus. Speaking of this, Forsyth says that 'It means that there was a close of strict Revelation, a specific revelation period, outside which the word revelation takes another sense, inferior and expository.'[6]

The use of the word 'revelation' in connection with knowledge, albeit in the qualified sense of the knowledge of faith (as distinct, for example, from Cartesian certainty), means that it operates as a 'success word': it presupposes that something has actually been conveyed from revealer to recipient. 'Revelation is . . . a "success word" (G. Ryle) which presupposes the reception of the communication (not, however, its acknowledgement – unless one regards the grace of God as irresistible).'[7] It is, to be sure, a success word only in an *a posteriori* sense: some seed has fallen on fertile soil, as a matter of historical and therefore contingent fact. We can speak of it so because it has happened, and been appropriated by the church whose distinctive form of life it makes possible. But the allusion to success, like all claims for a realisation of eschatology – especially in connection with the church – reveals the peril. What kind of success? What kind of theology of glory? An answer to those questions will occupy us for the remainder of the lecture.

---

[6] Forsyth, *The Principle of Authority*, p. 140.
[7] Schwöbel, *God. Action and Revelation*, p. 92.

III   *Anticipations of glory*

For all of its eschatological overtones, the orientation of the discussion of revelation as a category of systematic theology to Jesus means that the relation between past and present is the central focus of a discussion of the nature of revelation. Because the conclusion of the previous lecture was that revelation is that from which first scripture and then Christian tradition derive their distinctive character, it is with some features of biblical revelation that I shall present a survey of the scene. To begin with a slightly exaggerated contrast: in the Synoptic Gospels we obtain a view of revelation from the point of view of its first recipients; in the Fourth Gospel, one from the point of view of the later church.[8] There are a number of crucial expressions of revelation according to the shared if sometimes varying testimony of the Synoptic Gospels. It would be not a great exaggeration to say that whereas for John the whole of the life, death, resurrection and ascension of Jesus together and as a whole constitute the revelation of glory, the Synoptics concentrate attention on a number of crucial episodes. The first major event is without doubt the baptism of Jesus. In the Eastern Orthodox tradition this is often seen as a revelation of the Trinity, and indeed all three persons are economically involved in the story. But the focus of revelation is Jesus: it is he upon whom the Spirit descends, and he of whom it is said 'Thou art my beloved Son . . .' (Mk. 1.11, and parallels). Indeed, the words serve as a revelation by God the Father of who Jesus is.

The confession of Peter at Caesarea Philippi and the subsequent narrative of transfiguration are again declarative of the way in which God the Father reveals the Son: this time in terms of his destiny, and the kind of thing it means for him to be the Son of God. The confession of Peter is clearly revelatory, and while Mark characteristically leaves the later

---

[8] Here I am drawing on George Caird's point that the Fourth Gospel is distinctive because it is written from the vantage point of life in the church under the guidance of the Spirit. This accounts for the frequent expression of the fact that it was only after the Spirit was given that the disciples understood the point of things that Jesus said.

narrative to fill out the meaning, Matthew shows us the kind of revelation that it is. First, it is from God: 'flesh and blood has not revealed this to you, but my Father who is in heaven' (Mt. 16.17). But second, it is not transparent, and even as revelation requires interpretation. (This is a form of the openness with which I am concerned in the relation between revelation and the words which affect to express it.)[9] He is one whose sonship is expressed only in suffering and cross, and, before that and its outcome, Peter simply cannot comprehend what it means. This is in part because revelation is focused on the kind of saviour that Jesus is, and, like so much that is revelatory, upsets earlier expectations and preconceptions, and, although it is revelation, cannot be understood unless it is also shown to be such. (It is, in others words, revelation, although its success is at this stage of the process rather limited.)

All three evangelists interpret Peter's confession through the transfiguration when God affirms, in a way analogous to the baptism, both the confession and Jesus' interpretation of it. 'This is my beloved Son; listen to him' (Mk. 9.7). Again, there is both clear revelation and an incapacity of its recipients quite to understand what is happening. It is this latter and recurring feature which shows that the story is told from the point of view of those to whom it happened, and which indicates both the continuity with the Fourth Gospel and that Gospel's distinctive approach. Just as Caesarea Philippi was the revelation of the cross, the transfiguration clearly anticipates the resurrection, as Bultmann recognised albeit in a characteristically perverse way by claiming that it is a misplaced resurrection narrative.[10] Luke, if we may this time employ his account, makes it clear that it was to do with Jesus' fate, even though he too is concerned largely to see it from the point of view of those who were there. Moses and Elijah speak to him of the 'exodus' which he is to accomplish at Jerusalem (Lk. 9.31). The revelation of Jesus' glory as the Son of God, though

[9] See above, p. 67.
[10] It is asserted without argument in a number of places in Rudolf Bultmann, *Theology of the New Testament 1*, translated by K. Grobel (London: SCM Press, 1952), e.g. pp. 26–7.

here anticipated, will be complete only at the end of his ministry.[11]

It follows, then, that the third episode at which we must look is the outcome of the things adumbrated here. Here it is very difficult to retain a balance. In the first place, there seems little doubt that the resurrection is, from an epistemological point of view, the revelatory event *par excellence*, confirming as it does the revelations of the previous narratives. Despite all the appearances, despite the offence and the apparent failure, this *is* the Son sent for the salvation of the world. Here we can draw upon some of the things that Pannenberg has said about the resurrection as divine declaration of the significance of Jesus.[12] It is an eschatological event, and as such an anticipation of final revelation. The speeches in Acts, whether or not they express a primitive christology of messianic success after failure, make this point clear. Yet, in the second place, as that very allusion indicates, the resurrection is not revelation which in some way overturns the darkness of the cross, but rather establishes that, too, as revelation. This is important, for it maintains the secondary character of revelation. The revelation is of the suffering sonship of Jesus, that it is through his death above all that he is revealed to be the one that he is, the vehicle not primarily of revelation but of salvation, atonement in his blood: the restoration and realisation of the predestined human relationship to the father. By anticipation in baptism and transfiguration, in fullness at the cross, he is revealed as the one sent and anointed to bear the sin of the world and so to set his people free for God.

---

[11] 'It does not help much to discuss whether the story was originally a resurrection appearance or not, even if there are some overtones of resurrection . . . What has helped me both as student and preacher has been a glimpse . . . of Christ crucified as the Lord of glory, whose voice is the "I am" of the burning bush, and the thunder of Sinai, and the still small voice which Elijah hears in his despair. That is the meat of true theology.' Stuart G. Hall, 'Synoptic Transfigurations: Mark 9, 2–10 and Partners,' *King's Theological Review* X (1978), 41–4 (44).

[12] Pannenberg, *Jesus – God and Man*, especially Chapter 3.

IV   *Revelation and the glory of the crucified*

So far, then, as the Synoptic Gospels are concerned, the focus is on that part of the divine economy concerned with salvation. Very much the same is the case with John, and it can be argued that the definitive treatment of revelation in the New Testament is to be found in his Gospel. As I have suggested, in being centred on revelation from the point of view of the continuing church, it is of paramount importance for us. It is noteworthy that this writer is sometimes accused of Gnosticism, in view of the fact that he gives so much attention the concept of knowledge, the human and receptive side of the event of revelation. For a number of reasons, that charge cannot hold. While Gnosticism denies the goodness of the creation, John affirms it. While the former denies the human reality of Christ, John affirms it, not only with his programmatic statement of the incarnation of the Word, but with his characterisation of the human emotions and responses of the saviour.[13] While the former speaks of salvation by knowledge, the Gospel speaks of salvation by incarnation, the cross, resurrection and ascension, and the consequent sending of the Paraclete. As with the three other Gospels, what is revealed is primarily not knowledge, but salvation in Christ, though that includes epistemic dimensions.

There is much to be said for the use of this Gospel as a study in revelation. Its treatment of the knowledge of God in Christ is, indeed, by means of narrative, but narrative of a particular kind. The essential point is that revelation is treated relationally rather than merely narratively. This is important for reasons I have adduced in this and previous lectures. The narrative is not, without more ado, immediately – that is, without mediation – related to the reality of its readers, though the relation is direct. It may be that we are constituted, or, better, formed, at least in part, by the narratives so far as we take them to be definitive of our lives. But the problem with narrative, as we have seen above, is the problem of appealing to texts in the wrong way. Texts are not persons. They are written by people,

---

[13] We do not have to deny that in some of the things that he says this author also goes dangerously near to appearing to deny the humanity.

indeed, and are the mediators of a living relation to them. But unless more satisfactory account can be given of the fact that it is God who is the subject of their mediation, much is left hanging in the air, or remains in the realm of mere rhetoric. We should be alerted already to the distinct contribution that John has to make by his use of the idea of mutual indwelling. The knowledge of which he speaks is first of all the knowledge by acquaintance that is a function of the interrelatedness of persons.

John's account of the knowledge deriving from revelation is framed within an account of the relations of God with the world. These are diverse but unified. First is creation. The story John has to tell is prefaced with an account of the fact that the one of whom he is to speak is also the one through whom the world was made and holds together. Christ is the mediator of creation. Revelation may primarily be of salvation, but the saviour is the one through whom the world was made and is held in being. Second is incarnation. The mediator of creation becomes incarnate in Jesus Christ: the Word became flesh, and, indeed, in a revelatory way: 'we have beheld his glory' (Jn. 1.14). Revelation is thus at a datable time and place, tied offensively and unphilosophically, to a historical person.[14] And this revelation is unique: 'No one has ever seen God; the only Son, who is in the bosom of the Father, he has made him known' (1.18).

But, third, the one who makes God known is early identified as also the mediator of salvation. This is not simply epiphany, God manifest, though it is that. It is the epiphany of the one who is the mediator of God's salvation: the one who is the outcome of God's love for the world, 'the Lamb of God, who takes away the sin of the world' (1.29), the one who will be 'lifted up' (3.14, 8.28, 12.32), glorified, by the threefold saving event of death, resurrection and ascension, which together constitute the revelation of his glory. Through the whole, then, we are given a picture of a personal creator, whose relation to the world is defined from the beginning through his Son, and

[14] Paul's point is similar: see 1 Cor. 1.22f: 'For Jews demand signs and Greeks seek wisdom, but we preach Christ crucified . . .'.

whose sacrificial love is the means by which God's relation with his sinful people is re-established. It is through and as a function of all this that there is given, through revelation, what can only be called the knowledge of God, a knowledge which is both a personal relation and something that can be conveyed through words ('these are written that you may believe that Jesus is the Christ, the Son of God, and that believing you may have life in his name', 20.31).

When we examine the structure of this revelation, we shall see that it is trinitarian in a thoroughgoing but also distinctive way. One way of understanding it is to contrast its weighting of the actions of the persons of the Trinity with Barth's similar account. Barth's theology of revelation is, as is well known, strongly christological. Without denying that it is plainly trinitarian – that both Father and Spirit are given roles, as well as Jesus Christ who *is* revelation – there are a number of features that give cause for question. For example, is Barth right to describe Jesus Christ as revelation and the Father as revealer? In one respect he is, for that is clearly a feature of the Synoptic account which we have noted. The Father reveals, makes known, the Son to the otherwise half-comprehending disciples. But is there not also a sense in which it should be the other way round? We have already met the problem of Barth's tendency to underplay the significance of the humanity of Christ. It is accompanied by an equivalent failure to give due place and function to the Holy Spirit. For Barth, the Spirit is the 'subjective side in the event of revelation', 'God in his freedom to be present to the creature'.[15] This is Barth's equivalent of the Reformation concept of the internal word: God internally confirming for the believer the external word of scripture. The Spirit is the agent of the historicity of revelation.

Barth's theology of revelation not only represents a version of the Reformation teaching, but, as we saw in a previous lecture, also suggests a straining after precisely the kind of

---

[15] Barth, *Church Dogmatics* 1/1, pp. 449f. There is an interesting discussion of Barth's pneumatology by Robert W. Jenson in 'You Wonder where the Spirit Went', *Pro Ecclesia* 2 (1993), 296–304.

immediacy that is in this context rather suspect. In question is not only the matter of mediation that has met us throughout, but the weakness of much of the Western tradition in its treatment of the doctrine of the Holy Spirit, tending as it does to limit the Spirit's activity to the application to the believer of the benefits of Christ. Greater attention to this matter may at once suggest a more distinctive role for the Spirit and a more adequate conception of mediation. The reason is as follows. Revelation is, as we have seen, an eschatological concept: it is that which is awaited at the end of time, when we shall know as we are known. If there is any revelation in the midst of time, it will be because the Spirit, the agent of eschatological completeness and the one who perfects the creation, enables an anticipation to take place: so mediates revelation that we may say that the mysteries of God are made known in our time.

The difference of the Johannine account from the Synoptic is precisely to be found in the fact that the author writes from the point of view of those who live after the giving of the Spirit. The different viewpoint of John is his essentially churchly situation. The Synoptic Gospels show narratively that the disciples fail to understand what is before their eyes; there is revelation but not adequate apprehension. John explains the reason. The Spirit was not yet given, but now the Paraclete is with them (Jn. 7.39, cf. 12.16). Through the Spirit's gift, those who do not see are yet the ones, more blessed than Thomas who did, who are enabled to believe 'that Jesus is the Christ, the Son of God, and believing have life in his name'. That is the distinctive contribution of this Gospel, and it is the reason why John is able to show us the glory of the Christ not only at crucial moments of revelation, but in the whole of his life, from birth through to ascension.

The key is to be found in his more comprehensive theology of the Spirit. The Paraclete is the one whom the Father will send at the request of Jesus to provide something of that which he has been during his ministry, that and more. He will enable greater things to be done, and specifically will lead the church into all truth. 'All the truth' (16.13); that would appear to make the Spirit the agent of a great deal of revelation indeed. When, however, we read 'truth' in this Gospel, what we are reading about is Jesus Christ. Leading into all the truth means leading to Jesus. But that does not disqualify, as we shall see, a more universal meaning for the claim. We shall come later to the universal implications of a belief in the Spirit. First, however, we must complete our conversation with John.

It is important in this context to remember the oft-noted point that the Spirit is the self-effacing person of the Trinity: the one whose function is to point away from himself to Jesus. That is not a denial that the Spirit is revealed, but revealed as one *from* whom rather than *to* whom we look. The Spirit is revealed, that is to say, as the mediator of relation to God through Christ and *consequently* as the mediator of revelation. That is the heart of the theology of mediation that is being outlined in these lectures. Wherever there is revelation of any kind, there is the work of the creator and redeemer Spirit. But that is not John's primary concern, which is to show that revelation means glory, in the present, and it means Jesus. The Spirit reveals Jesus as the truth: as the revelation of God the Father. The complicating feature of the discussion here is that the one to whom the Spirit points is also self-effacing, but in a different way. Jesus is revealed as the one whose work is to do the will of another, of the one who sent him. We are not able to know this apart from the work of the Spirit; no revelation without inspiration. But Jesus is what it is all about. 'We have seen his glory, the glory of the only begotten Son of the Father, full of grace and truth' (1.14).

The glory is the glory of one who washes the feet of his disciples, is lifted up on the cross, and only through the trial of death is elevated to the glory that is reigning with the Father. It is important to realise this if we are to understand what kind of Father is revealed by the incarnate Son. If it is indeed true that those who have seen him have seen the Father, then it is the Father who is revealed in the incarnate humanity of this man glorified through humbling. There is thus a relation of likeness between Jesus and the one whom he reveals of the kind to rule out what has come to be called patriarchy. Jesus as revelation is revelation of one who is known through what he does and is. We might therefore say: the mediatory office of the Spirit is to point to, and in that sense, reveal the Son; that of the Son to reveal the Father.

As the question of a contrast with Barth has been raised in this lecture, it is worth asking at this stage whether Barth is right to emphasise as strongly as he does that God reveals himself, and whether the trinitarian structure of revelation might not have been better preserved in some such expression as the Son reveals the Father in and through the Holy Spirit. Such things certainly appear in Barth, but there is a tendency working against them suggesting that the Son reveals himself, with the result that the nature of the relation between Son and Father is obscured, and the work of the Spirit too closely located in the believer's subjective appropriation of revelation. In systematic theology, much hangs on the weighting of the various components of a locus. The point here is that without the revealing action of the Spirit, we shall not know Jesus as the way to God. But because the Spirit is not the Son, and the Son not the Father, there are differences of function and action, and therefore differences of mediation. The clue to the doctrine of revelation is accordingly to be found in unravelling the different patterns of mediation with which we are here concerned. There are, as we have seen, more than one, and it is their confusion that has caused so much of the recent difficulty with the doctrine. But the point with which to close this section is that there is no basic theological difference between the Synoptic and Johannine approach. In the latter, the part played by the Spirit is explicit; in the former, implicit, as one would expect in view of the difference of setting. But both are concerned with the mediation of eschatological glory: the glory of God in the face of Jesus Christ.

V   *Varieties of mediation, but one Lord*

And so we end, where we began, with a question of mediation. What are the conclusions to be drawn? The first points a major difference between a Christian theological epistemology and the traditional Greek principle which marked theology at least until and including Barth. It is the view that like can be known only by like: that is to say, that we can only know God by means of something Godlike.[16] This Aristotelian principle may well be the source of many of the structural weaknesses of Barth's remarkable theology.[17] It is often remarked that his theology of revelation gives the impression of suggesting ahistorical theophany. The Fourth Gospel suggests a more subtle interweaving of revelation not only through the like – he who has seen me has seen the Father – but its counterbalancing by a theology of revelation through otherness. The Father is indeed made known by Jesus, but as one who is greater than he (14.28), and so beyond all we can say and think: one revealed by humiliation and cross, but revealed none the less as other.

The second conclusion concerns the place of the Spirit in mediating revelation. A conception of mediation which is pneumatologically shaped enables us to ask in what sense can unlike be known by unlike? How far do we know things in their *otherness*?[18] Is the fact that God is revealed in the humanity of the incarnate Lord not another way of saying that we know God only as knowledge of him is *mediated* to us by that which is not God? And that this is the work of the Spirit, the eschatological other who summons all being to its true end? It is the distinctive action of the Spirit in revelation to make known through the humanity of Jesus both his glory and his coming from the one who sends him. In that respect, we must take leave of part of Professor Torrance's claim, cited with approval in the previous lecture, that 'the Word of Truth of the gospel

[16] It is also hardly surprising that since the time of Origen (Philo even) such desperate attempts have been made to secure the doctrine of the divinity of scripture.

[17] One of them is a tendency to read a doctrine of God too immediately out of christology, so that he is able to speak impressively of the humanity of God, but less so of the humanity of the incarnate Son. It is hardly surprising, in view of Barth's contention that God can only be known by God, that he is often accused of failing to give due weight to the human response to revelation, even though he does as a matter of fact affirm very strongly the reality of the human intellectual response.

[18] It may be that Hegel was seeking something like this, even though his final apotheosis of human knowing took away with the left all that he had given with the right.

. . . continuously begets the Church in history . . .'.[19] Rather, we must specify that it happens as the Word of Truth is mediated in the present by the Spirit of Truth. The one who realises – mediates – the truth of the gospel is the Spirit who enables Jesus to be known for who he is, the crucified, risen and ascended mediator of reconciliation with God.

But, third, can the development be taken farther? Can we, that is to say, move from mediation through the humanity of the incarnate Christ to some of the more general features of mediation with which we have been concerned? The wider revelatory work of the Spirit can be identified in two ways. The first concerns the way in which analogously to this, other created things may, through the Spirit, serve as mediators of the revelation that is Jesus Christ. Why should we not gladly accept the humanity of scripture as the vehicle of revelation? And why should not the created order and linguistic forms in general serve as media of revelation?[20] The second way of understanding the wider revelatory work of the Spirit takes us beyond divine revelation to the matter alluded to in connection with the Fourth Gospel, that of the universal implications of the claim that the Spirit is the one who leads into all truth. It is, I believe, legitimate to extend John's strictly christological construing of the concept of truth, so long as the extension is still christological. For John, the one incarnate in Jesus is the one through whom all things came to be and are held in being: Christ the creator. The co-eternal Word is thus the basis of any and all meaning as 'foundation': not only of the faith of the believer, but of the very possibility of knowledge of any kind. If Christ is the mediator of creation, then he is the basis of created rationality and therefore of human

---

[19] Above, p. 99.

[20] What is the relation between words and the Word? Augustine and Hegel both fall into the same Platonising error: the first concentrates too much on the inner meaning, and the communication of truth as inner enlightenment. The second makes inner enlightenment the locus of divine self-revelation, and comes to a similar Platonising assumption that the conceptual is a higher form of meaning than the 'representational'. They share with Barth the assumption that like is only known by like.

knowledge, wherever and whatever; we might say, of all human culture.[21] But that point must be developed pneumatologically also, so that all rationality, truth and beauty are seen to be realised through the perfecting agency of God the Spirit, who enables things to be known by human minds and made by human hands. Christ is indeed the Truth, but the truth becomes truth in all the different ways in which it is mediated by the Spirit. Pneumatology is thus the key to any adequate theology of revelation and of its mediation.

That leads to a final point, in recapitulation of the chief contention of these lectures. There are varieties of mediation, but there is one Lord. When we speak of revelation, we are speaking first of all of Jesus Christ, who thus forms the focus of all that we have to say. The centre of our attention is the glory of God in the face of Jesus Christ, and that glory is mediated in all kinds of ways: through the Bible, church traditions and confessions; through the creation that is from and to Christ; and even sometimes through the propositions of theologians, those scribes of the kingdom whose calling is to bring forth from their treasures things both old and new.

---

[21] Part of human culture, indeed a major part, is that many-faceted and indefinable thing called religion, and it must be stated here that a strongly trinitarian theology of revelation such as this could form the basis of a theology of religion which was able to affirm elements of truth in all kinds of religions without denying the soteriological and revelational universality of Jesus of Nazareth.

Select Bibliography
of Modern Works

Baillie, John. *The Idea of Revelation in Recent Thought* (New York: Columbia University Press, 1956).

Banner, Michael C. *The Justification of Science and the Rationality of Religious Belief* (Oxford: Clarendon Press, 1990).

Barr, James. 'The Problem of Fundamentalism Today', *Explorations in Theology 7. The Scope and Authority of the Bible* (London: SCM Press, 1980), pp. 65–90.

Barth, Karl. *Church Dogmatics*, translation edited by G. W. Bromiley and T. F. Torrance (Edinburgh: T&T Clark, 1957–69), volumes 1/1, 1/2, 3/1, 3/2 and 3/3.

Barth, Karl. *Fides Quaerens Intellectum. Anselm's Proof of the Existence of God in the Context of his Theological Scheme*, translated by I. W. Robertson (London: SCM Press, 1960).

Barth, Karl. *Protestant Theology in the Nineteenth Century: Its Background and History*, translated by B. Cozens and J. Bowden (London: SCM Press, 1972).

Berkeley, George. *Three Dialogues between Hylas and Philonous, in Opposition to Sceptics and Atheists* (1713; reprinted London: Dent, 1910).

Bettoni, Efrem. *Duns Scotus. The Basic Principles of his Philosophy*, translated by B. Bonansea (Westport, Connecticut: Greenwood Press, 1978).

Blumenberg, Hans. *The Legitimacy of the Modern Age*, translated by R. M. Wallace (Cambridge, MA, and London: MIT Press, 1983).

Buckley, Michael. *At the Origins of Modern Atheism* (New Haven and London: Yale University Press, 1987).

Cantor, Geoffrey. *Michael Faraday: Sandemanian and Scientist. A Study of Science and Religion in the Nineteenth Century* (London: Macmillan, 1991).

Coleridge, Samuel Taylor. *Collected Letters of Samuel Taylor Coleridge, Volume II. 1801–1806*, edited by E. L. Griggs (Oxford: Clarendon Press, 1956).

Coleridge, Samuel Taylor. *Confessions of an Enquiring Spirit* (1840; reprinted Philadelphia: Fortress Press, 1988).

Coleridge, Samuel Taylor. *The Table Talk of S. T. Coleridge*, introduced by H. Morley (London: Routledge, 1884).

Dalferth, Ingolf U. *Theology and Philosophy* (Oxford: Blackwell, 1988).

Dodd, C. H. *According to the Scriptures. The Substructure of New Testament Theology* (London: Collins, 1965. First edition 1952).

Dodd, C. H. *The Apostolic Preaching and its Developments* (London: Hodder & Stoughton, third edition, 1963).

'Dogmatic Constitution on Divine Revelation', *Vatican Council II. The Conciliar and Post-Conciliar Documents*, edited by A. Flannery OP (Leominster: Fowler Wright, 1975).

Downing, F. G. *Has Christianity a Revelation?* (London: SCM Press, 1964).

Einstein, Albert. *The World as I See It*, translated by Alan Harris (London: John Lane the Bodley Head, 1935).

Elert, Werner. *Der Ausgang der altkirchlichen Christologie* (Berlin: Lutherisches Verlagshaus, 1957).

Fichte, J. G. *Attempt at a Critique of all Revelation*, translated by Garrett Green (Cambridge: Cambridge University Press, 1978).

Forsyth, P. T. *The Principle of Authority* (London: Independent Press, 1952. First edition 1913).

Frei, Hans. *The Eclipse of Biblical Narrative. A Study in Eighteenth and Nineteenth Century Hermeneutics* (New Haven and London: Yale University Press, 1974).

Funkenstein, Amos. *Theology and the Scientific Imagination from the Middle Ages to the Seventeenth Century* (Princeton: Princeton University Press, 1986).

German, Terence J. *Hamann on Language and Religion* (Oxford: Oxford University Press, 1981).

Gunton, Colin E. 'Universal and Particular in Atonement Theology', *Religious Studies* 28 (1992), 453–66.

Gunton, Colin E. *The One, the Three and the Many. God, Creation and the Culture of Modernity. The 1992 Bampton Lectures* (Cambridge: Cambridge University Press, 1993).

Gunton, Colin E. 'Mozart the Theologian', *Theology* 94 (1991), 346–9.

Hall, Stuart G. 'Synoptic Transfigurations: Mark 9, 2–10 and Partners', *King's Theological Review* X (1978), 41–4 .

Harnack, Adolph. *History of Dogma*, Volume VI, translated by W. McGilchrist (London: Williams & Norgate, 1899).

Hauerwas, Stanley. *A Community of Character. Toward a Constructive Christian Social Ethic* (Notre Dame and London: University of Notre Dame Press, 1981).

Haymes, Brian. *The Concept of the Knowledge of God* (London: Macmillan, 1988).

Helm, Paul. *The Divine Revelation. The Basic Issues* (London: Marshall, Morgan & Scott, 1982).

Hodge, Charles. *Systematic Theology,* Volume 1 (reprinted, Grand Rapids: Eerdmans, 1989).

Jenson, Robert W. *God After God. The God of the Past and the God of the Future, Seen in the Work of Karl Barth* (Indianapolis and New York: Bobbs Merrill, 1969).

Jenson, Robert W. *Unbaptized God. The Basic Flaw in Ecumenical Theology* (Minneapolis: Fortress Press, 1992).

Kerr, Fergus. *The Later Wittgenstein and Theology* (Oxford: Blackwell, 1986).

Kierkegaard, Søren. *Philosophical Fragments,* translated by D. F. Swenson and H. V. Hong (Princeton: Princeton University Press, 1962).

Kuhn, Thomas. *The Structure of Scientific Revolutions* (Chicago: University of Chicago Press, second edition 1970).

Lindbeck, George. *The Nature of Doctrine. Religion and Theology in a Postliberal Age* (London: SPCK, 1984).

MacIntyre, Alasdair. *After Virtue. A Study in Moral Theory* (London: Duckworth, 1981).

McFague, Sallie. *Metaphorical Theology. Models of God in Religious Language* (London: SCM Press, 1983).

McGrath, Alister. *The Genesis of Doctrine. A Study in the Foundations of Doctrinal Criticism. The 1990 Bampton Lectures* (Oxford: Blackwell, 1990).

Moltmann, Jürgen. *Theology of Hope,* translated by J. W. Leitch (London: SCM Press, 1965).

Nebelsick, Harold. *The Renaissance, the Reformation and the Rise of Science* (Edinburgh: T&T Clark, 1992).

Newman, John Henry. *An Essay on the Development of Doctrine* (1845; reprinted Harmondsworth: Penguin Books, 1974).

Norris, Christopher. *Uncritical Theory. Postmodernism, Intellectuals and the Gulf War* (London: Lawrence & Wishart, 1992).

Pannenberg, Wolfhart. *Jesus – God and Man,* translated by L. Wilkins and D. Priebe (London: SCM Press, 1968).

Pannenberg, Wolfhart. *Systematic Theology Volume I,* translated by G. W. Bromiley (Edinburgh: T&T Clark, 1991).

Polanyi, Michael. *Personal Knowledge. Towards a Post-Critical Philosophy* (London: Routledge, second edition 1962).

Schwöbel, Christoph. 'Particularity, Universality and the Religions. Towards a Christian Theology of Religions', *Christian Uniqueness Reconsidered. The Myth of a Pluralistic Theology of Religions*, edited by Gavin D'Costa (New York: Orbis Books, 1990).

Schwöbel, Christoph. *God. Action and Revelation* (Kampen: Kok Pharos, 1992).

Spence, Alan. 'Christ's Humanity and Ours', Christoph Schwöbel and Colin E. Gunton, editors, *Persons, Divine and Human. King's College Essays in Theological Anthropology* (Edinburgh: T&T Clark, 1992), pp. 74–97.

Spence, Alan. 'Inspiration and Incarnation: John Owen and the Coherence of Christology', *King's Theological Review XII* (1989), 52–5

Surin, Kenneth. *The Turnings of Darkness and Light* (Cambridge: Cambridge University Press, 1989).

Thiemann, Ronald. *Revelation and Theology. The Gospel as Narrated Promise* (Notre Dame: University of Notre Dame Press, 1985).

Thunberg, Lars. *Man and the Cosmos. The Vision of St Maximus the Confessor* (New York: St Vladimir's Seminary Press, 1985).

Tillich, Paul. *Systematic Theology*, Volume 1 (London: Nelson, 1953).

Torrance, T. F. 'The Deposit of Faith', *Scottish Journal of Theology* 36 (1983), 1–28.

Torrance, T. F. *The Ground and Grammar of Theology* (Belfast: Christian Journals, 1980).

Torrance, T. F. *The Hermeneutics of John Calvin* (Edinburgh: Scottish Academic Press, 1988).

Torrance, T. F. *Transformation and Convergence within the Frame of Knowledge. Explorations in the Interrelations of Scientific and Theological Enterprise* (Belfast: Christian Journals, 1984).

Watson, Francis. *Text, Church and World. Biblical Interpretation in Theological Perspective* (Edinburgh: T&T Clark, 1994).

Whitehouse, W. A. *The Authority of Grace. Essays in Response to Karl Barth*, edited by Ann Loades (Edinburgh: T&T Clark, 1981).

Index of
Names and Subjects

Index of
Scriptural References